The Church before Christianity

THE CHURCH BEFORE CHRISTIANITY

Wes Howard-Brook

ORBIS BOOKS

Maryknoll, New York 10545

Founded in 1970, Orbis Books endeavors to publish works that enlighten the mind, nourish the spirit, and challenge the conscience. The publishing arm of the Maryknoll Fathers and Brothers, Orbis seeks to explore the global dimensions of the Christian faith and mission, to invite dialogue with diverse cultures and religious traditions, and to serve the cause of reconciliation and peace. The books published reflect the views of their authors and do not represent the official position of the Society. To learn more about Maryknoll and Orbis Books, please visit our website at www.maryknoll.com.

Copyright © 2001 by Wes Howard-Brook

Published by Orbis Books, Maryknoll, NY 10545-0308

Manufactured in the United States of America

Library of Congress Cataloging-in-Publication Data

Howard-Brook, Wes.
    The church before Christianity / Wes Howard-Brook.
        p. cm.
    Includes bibliographical references.
    ISBN 1-57075-403-9 (pbk.)
    1. Church—History of doctrines—Early church, ca. 30-600. I. Title.

BV600.3 .H69 2001
270.1—dc21

                                             2001036367

Contents

Acknowledgments

The idea for this book arose from the intersection of questions raised by many participants in church-based adult scripture classes which I have led in recent years and the work of numerous, vibrant Christian communities around the world. The questions come out of images I discuss from Revelation's vision of New Jerusalem or Acts' portrait of discipleship communities joyously sharing all things in common. One thing people want to know is, If church is supposed to be a completely alternative society to life in empire, then why has it become *so much less* today for most people? I am not a historian, and I leave it to others to address the implications of the question as far as they concern the transformation of "church" from small discipleship communities to global institutions more often supporting, rather than resisting, empire. But my work on the Bible and my awareness of the network of discipleship communities led me to feel called to respond to the second question. That is, What would it look like, in practical ways, to be church as the New Testament writers experienced and intended?

Some of the Christian communities taking this call seriously today I have experienced firsthand. Others I have only heard about, much as Paul heard of the churches in Rome and elsewhere (Rom. 1:1-15; cf. Eph. 1:15; Col. 1:1-4). I trust that for every one I have experienced or heard stories about, there are many others who practice the Good News without much publicity. Those I name here are thus just the tip of the iceberg: Jonah House in Baltimore; Open Door Community in Atlanta; Catholic Worker houses in Los Angeles, San Bruno (California), Tacoma (Washington), Brisbane (Australia), Vancouver (British Columbia), and Portland (Oregon); Church of the Savior and Sojourners in Washington, D.C.; Mamre Community in Sydney (Australia); the St. Therese sister parish in Chiapas (Mexico); Holden Village in North Cascades (Washington); First Christian Church in San Jose; First Congregational Church in Salem (Oregon); the simple way in Philadelphia; Center for Ministry at the Margins in Burlington (Washington); and St. Chiara's Community in Vancouver. There are also countless individuals and organizations whose ministry on the streets, in the jails, among the sick and in the woods reminds me that "being church" was not meant primarily to take place in a building by that name.

In keeping me sharply focused on the wonderfully radical nature of the first discipleship communities, I have no one to thank more than Ched Myers, who offered many excellent comments on the draft of this book and whose work and conversation over the years have been a constant source of inspiration and late-night fun. Other folks who provided helpful feedback on the manuscript include Johnny Zokovitch, Kate McMichael, and Theresa Hauser.

Here in Seattle, the members of our Eutychus Community, searching as we are for authentic discipleship while feeling constantly imprisoned within empire, keep this from being an academic exercise. And especially from within this close circle, I am grateful to my wife, Maggie, and son, Peter, whose love and penetrating questions encourage me to share with others how joyous and exciting the life of fidelity to God is intended to be. Perhaps it may seem trite to add, but I will anyway: I'm thankful to my dog Athena, who does God's will without trying, keeps me walking daily down by the lake, and helps me to listen for the Voice that is the true source of any wisdom that may come from my mouth or these pages.

Introduction

In their earliest days and years, the communities of discipleship that became known as "churches" were intended to be exciting, dynamic, Spirit-filled love feasts, celebrating, proclaiming, and witnessing to the Good News revealed in the living, dying, and rising of Jesus of Nazareth. Members were expected to throw their whole selves into it. The New Testament gives us a wide array of stunning images for the kind of commitment expected and given by people going forth together on the discipleship journey:

And immediately they left their nets and followed him. (Mark 1:18)

As shoes for your feet put on whatever will make you ready to proclaim the gospel of peace. (Eph. 6:15)

Come out of her, my people, so that you do not take part [in Babylon's sins]. . . . It is done! I am the Alpha and the Omega, the beginning and the end. To the thirsty I will give water as a gift from the spring of the water of life. Those who conquer will inherit these things, and I will be their God and they will be my children. (Rev. 18:4; 21:6-7)

Now the whole group of those who believed were of one heart and soul, and no one claimed private ownership of any possessions, but everything they owned was held in common. With great power the apostles gave their testimony to the resurrection of the Lord Jesus, and great grace was upon them all. There was not a needy person among them, for as many as owned lands or houses sold them and brought the proceeds of what was sold. They laid it at the apostles' feet, and it was distributed to each as any had need. (Acts 4:32-35)

Two thousand years later, much has changed. Whether you, the reader, are a minister, a church member looking for some inspiration or new ideas, or a seeker tentatively inquiring about the possibilities of life in the Christian community, perhaps one or more of the following statements may ring true to your own impression of churches today:

- Church seems boring. (My son's feeling!)

- Church is patriarchal: there's not room for the full participation of women.

- Church is homophobic: there's not room for the full participation of gays or lesbians.

- Church is authoritarian: people are told what to think and how to live.

- Church is intolerant of other viewpoints: sincere people of differing religious traditions are viewed and treated as "sinners" or at least as less than fully "saved."

- Church seems like a marketing scheme: it wants my money to build itself up and make itself powerful.

- Church seems fluffy: it hasn't the "guts" to take on the difficult social and economic issues of our time, either with words or actions.

No church in our world could claim all these attributes, and yet many Christian assemblies and denominations radiate some of these characteristics. We will look briefly at how it got this way and why it seems to stay this way, but *the premise of this book is that none of these characteristics could be found in the idea of "church" before what became known as "Christianity."*

I write this not as someone with or seeking answers to problems in the church, but as a person who, although intertwined with "church" at many levels of my life, regularly experiences a "disconnect" between my experiences of church and what I think it was meant to be and what is desperately needed in our wounded world. I am a member of a local Roman Catholic parish in Seattle, Washington, one considered by many to be "progressive" in many ways. My wife, Maggie, is one of several lay presiders who share leadership with the priest-pastor. We openly embrace gays and lesbians. We have a degree of cultural diversity among our membership. We have a vibrant and growing number of young adults and young families. And yet we are a long way from expressing the kind of church intended by the earliest disciples. Only a small number of members participate beyond weekly or holiday liturgies or personal sacramental moments (marriages, baptisms, funerals). Our economic and social lives are fragmented, a function in part of our residence in over fifty zip codes in the greater Puget Sound area. And, like most people in the United States today, we are caught up in the busyness into which we are seduced by the global economy and the pursuit of the privileged lifestyle our relatively high education and professional skills make available for many of us.

Maggie and I are also involved with church at a more intimate level as members of Eutychus Community. The community is named for the character in Acts 20 who falls asleep during one of Paul's long sermons and drops three stories through an open window, only to be picked up and dusted off by Paul, who, having determined that "there is still life in him," continues preaching until dawn. Our informal motto is "we may fall asleep, but there's still life in us!" Eutychus Community consists of (at the moment of this writing) thirteen adults who come from diverse cultural and Christian backgrounds. We are Roman Catholic, Lutheran, and United Church of Christ. We are Hispanic, Filipino, African, Jewish, and various flavors of European ancestry. We are church workers (ordained and lay), parents, office workers, and artists. We meet weekly for prayer, Bible study, and potlucks, and seasonally (Lent and Advent) for public prayer and acts of faithful resistance to injustice. And yet there is something missing: given each of our separate work and social lives, our lives intersect only with great scheduling difficulty. We yearn for more intimacy, more commitment, more exciting experiences of being church together, but find the road between here and there filled with barriers and dead ends.

Finally, as a Bible teacher and writer, I am also involved with "church" through the informal, ecumenical network of small communities, organizations, and publications that provide "strength for the journey" (the motto of the ecumenical Christian magazine *The Other Side*). Unbeknownst to many Christians, our world is dotted with many exciting experiments in being church in ways that are rooted in the practice and ideals of our earliest Christian ancestors. The network of Catholic Worker communities founded first by Dorothy Day in the 1930s as houses of hospitality amidst the ravages of the Depression has grown and adapted into a wonderful diversity of local communities around the world. The Church of the Savior in Washington, D.C., has been a fertile source of house churches planted for specific missions of service to the poor and marginalized. Churches grounded in the experience of the civil rights movement have evolved into vibrant communities of faith bustling with cultural diversity. The "base community" movement in Latin America has inspired others in both the Two Thirds World and in the West to attempt to be church locally while remaining engaged with the social and political realities surrounding them. And there has always been, from the earliest days of church, an informal springing up of local communities guided by a sense that the Spirit has called them together for celebration and for mission, with no denominational or other traditional support. Through work for common causes (for an end to war, to economic oppression, to racism), these communities have found and supported one another. And yet there is often still something missing. While our modern systems of global communication have assisted us in some ways in keeping track of each other's activities, we remain largely isolated from one another. We pray for and wish each other well, and some folks even get a chance to visit other communities once in a while, but our physical connections are very limited, and we can rarely come together as a movement to discern the Spirit's call.

I share these pieces of my own search for "church" because this book flows directly out of these experiences, struggles, and dreams. In my years (since 1988) teaching the Bible to ministry students and members of congregations, both Catholic and Protestant, I often hear in words or see in puzzled or anguished faces the sense expressed by Nicodemus to Jesus in John's Gospel, "How is it possible?" (John 3:9). I believe that many people are yearning for a powerful experience of Christian community, want to be part of an authentic, prayerful, celebrating assembly that looks the world as it is in the eye and offers Good News, but they don't know how to get from here to there. When we study the ancient foundational texts of the New Testament, people's hearts open up to the adventure, beauty, and joy presented there, but their experience of church seems so removed from the vision they hear proclaimed that they wonder if it is not too late in the day to dream of being church as our ancestors tried to be themselves.

I hope in this book to address this yearning and this struggle. Before I found myself called into my current ministry, I spent six years as an attorney, two of those as a counsel to the United States Senate Judiciary Committee. That committee is responsible for, among other things, issues of constitutional law, civil rights, and criminal justice in our society. "Hot button" issues such as abortion, gun control, and capital punishment were discussed. When people want to determine how to move forward on important life-and-death concerns such as these but find themselves sharply and often emotionally divided, they frequently turn to their foundational texts for guidance. The Constitution's Second Amendment (right to bear arms), Eighth Amendment (prohibition of "cruel and unusual punishment"), and so-called penumbral rights (right to privacy established by the Supreme Court but not explicitly stated in the Constitution) are debated, not as if they were freshly composed statements but as ancestral inheritances.

The "original intent" of the founders is frequently invoked in such discussions. For instance, how is the principle that a people struggling to establish and maintain their freedom and independence from a powerful military empire had a right to defend themselves with muskets related to the possession today of semiautomatic weapons or handguns? With important questions such as this, the Judiciary Committee would frequently find itself conducting historical inquiries into the intent and practices of our American ancestors. In sum, they were trying to find out what it meant to be "United States citizens" before there was a powerful nation called "America."

This book will attempt to do for "church" what the Judiciary Committee debates do for constitutional and other civic questions, but with fewer lobbyists. It will focus on the New Testament images and stories of being "church" in the first generation or two after Jesus.

"Church" or "Churches"?

As a matter of historical fact, we must admit at the outset that there never has been such an entity as "the church" in the sense of a single community, institution, or theological perspective that embraced all who claimed to be disciples of Jesus. Raymond E. Brown showed in his aptly entitled book *The Churches the Apostles Left Behind* that each community was an ongoing experiment in walking the journey in uncharted territory. Without a centralized authority—either personal or institutional—to decide matters of theology and practice, individual discipleship groups were left on their own, under the guidance of the Holy Spirit and their own experience and insight, to determine the meaning of "church." At some level, this has always been the case, regardless of official denominational rules and theology. For instance, the most centralized of Christian traditions, the Roman Catholic, has evolved a great diversity of practices in its thousands of local communities across the world's cultural contexts. Some specific practices have been challenged by Vatican officials, and occasionally individual priests, theologians, or even congregations have been censured for moving too far from official norms. But even the Vatican cannot be in every church on every Sunday.

Thus, to speak of "the church" is to acknowledge that we are not talking about uniformity of practice, either in the ancient world or in ours. Rather, what I intend to show are the elements of being church that seem to have been shared by a diversity of New Testament writers and their communities. At the same time, we will see how the struggle to maintain this emerging, shared perspective on being church focused primarily on one issue: How much does being church put us at odds with the ways of our neighbors? Clearly, the New Testament shows that there was not in fact a uniform response to this difficult question. But there does seem to have been one widespread viewpoint, as we shall see, grounded in the very use of the term "church" (Greek *ekklēsia*) to refer to the discipleship community. For now, the "bottom line" is that *ekklēsia*, a Greek concept referring to the political assembly, means literally "called out." *The church is a community of people called out of empire by the Spirit of Jesus to live as an alternative society in the midst of the imperial world.* Because it is a key term used throughout this book, it is worth stopping for a moment to consider what I mean by "empire." Broadly speaking, "empire" refers to an organized system of power used against the many for the benefit of the few, which seeks legitimacy by claiming divine mandate. From Abraham's call to come out of the Mesopotamian empire, to the call of the first followers of Jesus to come out of the Roman empire, this has been the consistent biblical mandate throughout history. Being "church," then, meant fulfilling this ancient mandate in a new time and in new places. It is the contours of this viewpoint that will make up the bulk of this book.

Before Christianity

Many readers may realize that this book's title is a conscious echo of the landmark work by Albert Nolan, *Jesus before Chris-*

tianity, first published in 1976 and revised in 1992. Nolan's premise was that the radical preaching and practice of Jesus had been so watered down and domesticated over the centuries that it had been robbed of its power to transform a world in great need of healing and salvation. His opening chapter presented a summary diagnosis of the world's ills, a description that is as apt today as it was a quarter century ago, only the symptoms he named have grown worse and the patient sicker. Nolan's investigation looked at Jesus in Jesus' own context, the villages and roads of first-century Palestine, in confrontation with the Jerusalem Temple and its officials and supporters. What emerged was a portrait of a man sent by God to proclaim and celebrate the Good News of God's reign (kingdom) among the poor and those who would become identified with the poor so as to take part in this new divine work. He showed how Jesus' message was deeply concerned with the day-to-day economic, political, and social realities of peasants and other poor people in Palestine. It offered not a "pie-in-the-sky" promise of afterlife bliss but a way to live joyously, lovingly, and compassionately in God's abundant grace *here and now*. In portraying this Jesus, Nolan made clear why he was such a threat to the defenders of the status quo and therefore why he was killed: not as "God's will" in the sense that God wanted Jesus to die, but in that Jesus remained faithful to his divinely inspired vision no matter what the consequences.

Nolan wrote his powerful book with passion and commitment. Its persuasive power came not just from its scholarly analysis of texts but from the context of Nolan's life as a European Dominican priest working in South Africa during apartheid. From his down-to-earth position in solidarity with people struggling daily to claim lives of dignity and freedom, he could see aspects of Jesus' life and preaching that were sometimes hidden from writers living "above the fray."

I will not claim the marks of solidarity and suffering which properly belong to Nolan and the people for whom he wrote. But I present this snapshot because one thing Nolan did that is beginning to become accepted even among more academic scholars is to recognize that, in the words of a Haitian proverb, "We see from where we stand." Nolan stood among poor people oppressed by a powerful empire. He looked at Jesus and saw someone in a similar situation. It was not a matter of "projection" or wishful thinking. Jesus truly stood among the poor, who were indeed oppressed. It was Nolan's vantage point that allowed him to look past the encrustations of "Christianity" to the Jesus who lived and walked among people similar to those whose lives surrounded Nolan, too.

I walk in a very different territory. Although my land is also filled with poor people struggling to live lives of dignity and freedom, they are more hidden than those in Nolan's South Africa, perhaps as they were from whites in Johannesburg, who were shielded from the shantytowns. My environment is urban and educated. I write as a lay Catholic whose ministry is supported and affirmed by parishes and dioceses, as well as by Protestant congregations. Although we don't live in luxury as defined by American popular (corporate) culture, we are not in want of any of the necessities of life and we reap enormous privilege as educated citizens of empire of the dominant racial category. My life is not like that of Jesus nor like that of Nolan and his people.

It is, however, I believe, like that of many followers of Jesus after the first Easter. What began as a movement among peasants in Palestine quickly became an urban phenomenon among the cities of the Roman empire. Most scholars would agree that virtually all the New Testament documents were written by and for people living in cities, many of whom were well off. Although the Gospels tell stories of Jesus among village people, the written texts were intended for a very different audience. Many Greco-Roman city dwellers had grown up in villages only to be forced into city life through Roman land-grabbing or slave-taking. Having been ripped out of their familiar social setting, their struggle was now not to raise grain and feed their families and animals, but to find physical and emotional security and meaning amidst the often dangerous and lonely world of the city. Those who were baptized into discipleship communities were hoping that they would find there a place of support and solidarity. In being baptized, they were, to some degree, rejecting the "religions" (in the literal sense of the Latin *religio*, meaning "to bind together again") offered by the surrounding cultural milieu. The key question was, How much of that surrounding world was inconsistent with their baptism? In other words, what did it mean to be "the people of God," "the body of Christ," that is, "the church"?

Neither Jesus nor any of the New Testament writers ever refer to this movement as "Christianity." Indeed, the term "Christian" was used as a pejorative term by opponents of the movement. It is found in the New Testament in only three places. In Acts 11:26, Luke notes in passing that "it was in Antioch that the disciples were first called 'Christians.'" He doesn't say who called them by this name or why. Acts' own narrative quickly moves on to another subject. Late in the book, King Agrippa says to Paul, who stands before him in chains giving testimony about his own commitment to the Way of Jesus, "Are you so quickly persuading me to become a Christian?" (Acts 26:28). Paul's response does not deny the evangelical tone and intent of his speech, but does not use the term "Christian" at all. The final place where the term is used is in the relatively late letter called First Peter. The author's purpose is to strengthen those who are finding the cost of discipleship too high. In trying to help them walk the line between their faith and the way of empire, he says to them, "Yet if any of you suffers as a Christian, do not consider it a disgrace, but glorify God because you bear this name" (1 Pet. 4:16).

These brief verses are as close as the New Testament comes to discussing "Christianity." By the end of the first century and the beginning of the second, though, structures were developing among some discipleship communities. Offices of "bishop" (overseer) and "presbyter" (elder) were being established. Creedal statements were being formed. Manuals of ritual were developing. Sociologist Max Weber has argued that it is the nature of charismatic movements to develop rituals and institutional forms if they are to survive. Structures of some sort had to develop if the message of Jesus was to be told across the long haul of time and space. Some writers advocated structures which allowed for various degrees of assimilation to the Roman way of life. At the same time, second-century writers such as Ignatius of Antioch, Polycarp of Smyrna, and Clement of Alexandria—city dwellers all—show a stubborn resistance to accommodation to Roman economic, military, and ideological practices. Both the voices of assimilation and those of resistance came to rely on the witness of those first disciples whose memories and experiences formed the earliest narratives of what it meant to be church. I hope that my location as a disciple living an urban life amidst a powerful empire might help shed some light on these earliest images and experiences of being church, light that might in turn help the churches today to recover some of their vocation, so that the gospel can truly be proclaimed and lived in a world yearning desperately for some good news.

The Church Then and the Church Now

If we are to learn anything valuable from looking at the stories of the earliest discipleship communities, we must consider both what is similar across the millennia and what is different. I have noted that one similarity is the effort to remain faithful to the vision of Jesus living in cities amidst the powerful countervailing forces of empire, whether ancient Roman or the current form wielded by global corporations and the nation-states that serve them. One major difference to which I have alluded is the sheer passage of time, that is, the existence and history of Christianity. We cannot pretend to be starting from scratch as if Christianity had not been changed from a force in *resistance to* empire into the religion *of* empire. We cannot avoid the dark history of Crusades, Inquisition, and conquest. At the same time, we cannot ignore the brighter history of holy women and men whose openness to the Spirit produced fresh movements of discipleship, a great library of writings, and a legacy of inspiring Christian art and music. For us to bind together the faith experience of the early church with that of churches today requires not a denial of history or a collapsing of social and cultural differences, but a recognition that the true church, wherever and whenever it is found, is first and foremost a work of the Holy Spirit. If "the gates of hell" cannot prevail against the church, it is not because of human effort or holiness, but because it is God's own Spirit that calls discipleship communities into being and sustains them on the Way with gifts of compassion, strength, hope, and love.

Because there is one Holy Spirit and not many, the church, despite the differences in culture, politics, and society, remains called to an unchanging mission: the proclaiming and living out of God's reign within the context of empire. Similarly, the basic issues that faced our faith ancestors are very close to the questions with which this chapter began. What is the nature of authority in the church? What is the mission? Should the church be "marketing" itself in competition with other religions? What practical, economic, and social commitments are members making to love and support one another? How do we find strength for the long haul, until the day when God's reign is fully revealed?

We will consider the light the New Testament texts shed on these questions as follows. In doing so, we must be careful to remember that the New Testament expresses a combination of memory and exhortation, experience and hope. Just as official church documents or collections of sermons from churches in our time start from the actual faith lives of local church members and then seek to encourage deeper commitment to the gospel way of life, the texts we will consider describe *both* what the church *was* and what it *should* be when it is faithful to its call. We will therefore examine their vision for the church in light of *some* experiences in urban congregations scattered around the Mediterranean region.

Chapter 1: What Is "Church"?: The Roots of Ekklēsia *in Israel, Greece, and Rome.* Jesus was passionately committed to restoring the social bonds among God's people that were undermined by the economic and ideological disruptions of the Roman empire and Judean collaborators. However, his work of community building did not involve starting "churches," at least not in the sense of using the Greek word *ekklēsia*.* Among the rural poor in Palestine, historical images associated with *ekklēsia* would not have had the same resonance as they did for city dwellers. But New Testament writers such as Luke, John of Patmos, Paul, and the other epistle authors writing for urban communities use the term over one hundred times. We will begin by looking at the relationship between *ekklēsia* and Israel's descriptions of its own congregation, both in Hebrew Scripture and beyond. Next we will explore the origins of the term *ekklēsia* itself in the Athenian democratic assembly and other Greek practice, and how that history affected the New Testament idea of church. Finally, we will consider how both the Jewish and Christian notions of a "holy assembly" intersected in the context of the Roman empire, where the *familia*—the patriarchal family—was the primary unit of society.

Chapter 2: Singing a New Song: Prayer and Worship in the Ekklēsia. Most Christians today would likely think of Sunday worship as the primary, if not the exclusive, church activity in which they participate on a regular basis. The early church's liturgy, like ours, was not practiced in a vacuum, however. It took place within a world abounding in religious celebrations, both public and private. We will explore how the church's liturgy was explicitly aimed at proclaiming political allegiance: God and Jesus (not Caesar) reign supreme! In a similar way, other church rituals and disciplines, such as baptism, Eucharist, footwashing, and forgiveness were intended to develop and foster a sense of loving intimacy and trust among the *ekklēsia*'s members through which

---

* Matthew 16:18 and 18:15-21 are the only Gospel passages in which the term is used. Given the absence of these passages from Matthew's primary source text, the Gospel of Mark, one can fairly question whether Jesus himself made these statements or whether the author of Matthew's Gospel inserted them to offer teaching about forgiveness to his own discipleship community.

people would truly see and treat one another as sisters and brothers. Finally, the community's nonliturgical prayer—along with disciplines such as Bible study—was intended to provide clarity that would help "discern spirits" and refocus Christians on the gospel Word in the midst of numerous other voices clamoring for allegiance.

Chapter 3: Brothers and Sisters in Christ: The Ekklēsia *as God's Household.* One of the key aspects of Jesus' message that the church strove to live was the equality of all persons in God's sight. Paul's emancipation proclamation, "There is no longer Jew or Greek, there is no longer slave or free, there is no longer male and female; for all of you are one in Christ Jesus" (Gal. 3:28), called for a community in radical opposition to the hierarchies of both Hellenistic and Roman societies. We will consider how the language of *kinship*—referring to fellow believers as "sister" and "brother"—was intended to bond church members into a new "family" that would support one another in good times and bad times. Economically, this meant living according to Jesus' proclamation of sabbath and jubilee: the wiping out of debts and consequent living out of a sense of God's gift of abundance rather than empire's carefully controlled scarcity. We will explore examples of how the church endeavored not only to preach but to live in its daily life through the biblical tradition of "covenant economics."

Chapter 4: Ministry. An incredible amount of emotion and thought has been spent, especially in recent years, in arguments over ordained versus lay and male versus female "rights" in ministry. We may or may not be surprised to find that the earliest *ekklēsiai* knew nothing about "ordination" or Christian "priests." We will examine several cultural models to which the church responded in shaping its ministry, including the biblical inheritance from Israel, the metaphor of the body from Greek philosophy, and the Roman imperial cult. In terms both of model and function, we will see that ministries were not narrowly defined as ecclesial (i.e., "churchly") activities, but included the key practices of compassionate service and prophetic public witness in the world. They were intended to be practiced not with grim determination or on the perennial edge of burnout, but with the joyous sense of providing "food" for the journey for both servant and those served.

Chapter 5: The Mission in the World. Not until Paul the Pharisee hit the road had there been a Jewish mission to evangelize others into joining God's people. Today, questions of mission are necessarily overlaid with a history of conquest and imperialism, as well as an abhorrence by liberals of an overzealous effort to "impose" one's religious views on others. Once again, the early church knew nothing of imperial conquest in the name of Jesus, nor did it have the social power to "impose" anything on anyone. Instead, we find mission consisting of four central tasks set before the disciples by Jesus: preaching Good News throughout the world, healing the sick and disabled, ridding people of "unclean" or evil spirits that kept them from being truly free, and witnessing publicly to God's work in the life of the *ekklēsia* and the world.

Chapter 6: The Early Ekklēsia *Today: An Experimental Model for Discussion and Prayer.* There has never been a "perfect" church, nor will there ever be one. At the same time, there are some faith communities and institutions that are experimenting in exciting and joyous ways with being church. We will conclude with an exercise in imagination that might stimulate your own experiments where you live and attempt to practice discipleship in community with others.

1

What Is "Church"?

The Roots of Ekklēsia *in Israel, Greece, and Rome*

The church, like Jesus, did not arise out of nothing. The New Testament is but the final chapter in a collection of remembrances and stories of people living amidst surrounding cultures who felt called by the Creator to a way of life different from their neighbors. Thus, the first place to look is in the books of the Hebrew Scriptures to find what they say about what it meant to be "church."

The Assembly of Israel

Of course, to use the word "church" in reference to ancient Israel is anachronistic. Yet the third-century B.C.E. Greek translation of the Hebrew Scriptures known as the Septuagint frequently used the word *ekklēsia* to refer to the Israelite assembly. It also uses the more familiar word *synagōgē* (from which we get the word "synagogue") more than two hundred times. This word, as verb and noun, means "to gather" and "gathering." As with the modern use of "church," it can refer both to the *people* and to a *building* in which people gather for prayer and worship. Let's consider the roots of these terms in both the Hebrew language and in the stories of ancient Israel.

In the narratives of the Exodus journey from captivity in Egypt to settlement in the land of Canaan, the Hebrew word *ᶜedah* is generally used to refer to the entire body of people. This word is often translated as "congregation" (e.g., Exod. 12:19 NRSV). Also used regularly is the Hebrew *qahal*, translated as "assembly." This word is found mostly in biblical texts likely written after the Babylonian exile. It therefore tends to express the views of the literate elite concerned with restoring Jerusalem to its preexilic place as the central site of YHWH* worship. The Septuagint translators apparently did not understand there to be a clear distinction between the terms, as both can be rendered in Greek as either *ekklēsia* or *synagōgē*. In some situations in Hebrew Scripture, *qahal* seems to refer to a judicial body drawn from the wider *ᶜedah*, for example, Leviticus 4:13: "If the whole congregation [*kol-ᶜadath*] of Israel errs unintentionally and the matter escapes the notice of the assembly [*ha-qahal*] . . . " However, the Septuagint uses *synagōgē* for both terms in this verse. This likely reflects the urban, Hellenistic cultural usage of the Alexandrian scribes responsible for the Septuagint translation.

Both Hebrew terms can be used in secular or religious contexts, for example, an "assembly [*qehal*] of evildoers" (Ps. 26:5) or a "congregation [*ᶜadath*] of bees" (Judg. 14:8). We can see that just as Jesus' followers chose a word to refer to the assembly of disciples that was used originally in a secular context, so too Israel's scribes designated their religious assembly using language adapted from life's wider context.

---

*I use the term *YHWH* rather than *Yahweh* to underscore the sacredness attached by Israel to the divine name, which was never pronounced by Israelites or later by Jews.

The Exodus stories offer an idealized conception of Israel as an assembly or congregation: with few exceptions, the entire body acts together as the people of YHWH. Indeed, among the most powerful stories in Exodus and Numbers are those in which certain individuals act outside of the communal will, usually as determined by Moses and Aaron as YHWH's mediators. One of the purposes of the long narrative of the wilderness wanderings is to make precisely this point: to be true to the covenant, the people must be united in intention and action. The consequences of dissent are rebellion, violence, and eventually the destruction of the entire community.

This was certainly the understanding of those who, hundreds of years later, experienced and reflected on the wrenching loss of Jerusalem and its Temple during their years of exile in Babylon. Either when kings led the people astray by practicing the religions of other peoples or when ordinary "persons of the land" confused the way of YHWH with the ways of, say, the Canaanite god Baʿal, destruction was inevitable. The expression of the first experience is seen in the so-called Deuteronomistic History, covering the doings of judges and kings from Exodus to exile and comprising the books from Joshua to Second Kings. The expression of the second experience is found in the books of Ezra, Nehemiah, and Chronicles, written to provide a basis for the reestablishment of Jerusalem and its Temple system after Babylon was defeated and the exiles allowed to return to Canaan.

Both sets of writings, like Exodus–Numbers, are highly schematized narratives. They reflect the views of educated priests and scribes whose identities were deeply entwined with Jerusalem and the Temple. But what of the great majority of people who lived in the villages and towns of Canaan outside the urban core? How would they have thought of themselves as part of the "assembly" or "congregation" of YHWH?

Because these people were largely illiterate farmers, nomads, and local merchants and traders, we can have little direct evidence of their sense of belonging to a religious community. There are, though, some things we can know and hints of others. As with people virtually everywhere, the primary unit of daily life was the household, known in Hebrew as *bet ʾab*, "father's house." In Israel's narratives of origins, we hear the stories of largely self-sufficient households such as those of Abraham and Sarah, Isaac and Rebekah, and Jacob and Rachel (and Leah). These stories tell us little about "ordinary" life, but focus on the key moments when the household found self-sufficiency difficult if not impossible. Those key moments centered on the most basic issues of life: finding food, having children, and attending to the needs of the dying and the dead. For instance, we see both Abraham and Isaac lying about their wives to powerful urban rulers in times of famine in order to protect their own lives (Gen. 12:10-20; 20:1-18; 26:1-13). Similarly, we see tremendous struggles over children and identity, as barren wives and conniving relatives threaten the ability of the first families to settle in the land promised to them by God (e.g., Gen. 21:9-21; 24:1-2). Although the story world (i.e., the world reflected in the stories themselves) of these Genesis narratives is hundreds of years earlier than the glory days of Israel's monarchy, the storytellers' own worlds are much later, perhaps finally as late as the exile and after. They reflect a desire to remind people of the basic unit of society in which choices about religion and culture take place. Temple priests can recite all the commandments they wish in the name of God, but unless people are faithful to God at the most local levels, the entire society will go astray.

As Genesis suggests, people could not remain self-sufficient as isolated households. They needed to form economic and mutual security alliances with others. The central question, then as now, is: How much do such alliances respond to or resist one's sense of the divine order? Genesis shows us the struggle between Abraham's experience of being called by a God eventually known as YHWH and his embeddedness first in Mesopotamian and later in Canaanite city-state religions. He heard the voice of a God who drew him away from places that celebrated the sacredness of cities and their human rulers. Yet he knew that there were times in which the challenge of living totally apart from those systems was great. Genesis ends, of course, with Abraham's great-grandson, Joseph, as virtual ruler of all Egypt, whose authority and stature draw his own father and brothers into the vortex of imperial power along with him. What seems to be a happy ending is but the preface to their own descendants' slavery and yearning to return to the land of God's promise.

The Exodus story provides the means for this people to live according to their understanding of the divine will: the terms of the covenant found not only in Exodus but also in Leviticus and Deuteronomy. It is in these books that we find the greatest concentration by far of the words *qahal* and *ʿedah*. In these narratives, a multigenerational family has become the congregation/assembly of Israel. But the people obviously were intended to live not in the wilderness but in the Land. The stories of this transition are anticipated in Deuteronomy and told in Joshua and Judges. Much of Deuteronomy was written after the exile, projecting that experience back into the initial transition into the Land. In it we hear Moses repeatedly warning the people not to forget their experience of the God who called them out of empire and into freedom. The warnings frequently include strong admonitions not to marry the locals, for fear that the Israelites' commitment to the covenant would be watered down or lost altogether (e.g., Deut. 7:1-6). Deuteronomy recognizes what Joshua will narrate: the difficulty of living among people who worship other gods—and thus practice different social and economic relationships—while remaining true to one's own deity and that deity's lifeways.

In the book of Joshua, we hear stories of the partial conquest of the indigenous people of Canaan. Joshua leads "all Israel" in battle against various kings in fulfillment of God's commands. In his final speech, Joshua, like Moses in Deuteronomy, warns the people of the price of failure to live completely in accordance with the covenant with YHWH. The story narrates a covenant renewal ceremony in which "all Israel" recommits itself as a body to worship YHWH. But the kicker is found in Joshua's reply: "Then put away the foreign gods that are among you, and incline your hearts to YHWH, the God of Israel" (Josh. 24:24). Even as the people proclaim their loyalty to YHWH, they are found with "foreign gods" in their midst!

After Joshua's death, the Israelites faced one of the primary threats of settled people: military invasion. The book of Judges tells stories of God's calling forth heroic figures, both male and female, to lead the people in these times of war. If we read these stories carefully, we gain a helpful glimpse into the life of Israel between their household origins and the time of Jerusalem-based empire. During this period, the social units we hear most about are those situated between household and nation: the tribe and its clans. The clan (Hebrew *mishpachah*) is described by Norman Gottwald as "a protective association of extended families." Although the clans were said to have been numbered during the Exodus (Num. 1-4, 26), we don't see people actually living at this social level until Judges. When leaders and soldiers are sought, it is the ranks of clans that are searched. The clan structure of local households in mutual security alliance comprised the self-sufficient, hill-country village life that was Israel's basic alternative to the structure of the Canaanite city-states in the Palestinian plains. Clan-based villages probably comprised between fifty and five hundred or so persons, plus animals and properties, in living space occupying between one-half and two and one-half acres. Through shared economic and social interactions by day and sacred storytelling by night, the clan bound people together into a common sense of divinely authorized purpose.

The larger unit, the tribe, was almost certainly more of an abstraction in daily life, something like our experience of being residents of "California" or "New York." Except as taxpayers or when dealing with other laws, our sense of being part of a particular state does not greatly influence our identity. Similarly, the role of "tribe" in Israel during this period was to give people a sense of bonding at the level beyond that of ordinary life, in those situations when circumstances demanded that people act together in wider circles of connectedness. For instance, in Deborah and Barak's victory song, we hear:

> From Ephraim they set out into the valley,
>   following you, Benjamin, with your kin;
> from Machir marched down the commanders,
>   and from Zebulun those who bear the marshal's
>   staff;
> the chiefs of Issachar came with Deborah,
>   and Issachar faithful to Barak;
>   into the valley they rushed out at his heels.
> Among the clans of Reuben
>   there were great searchings of heart.
> Why did you tarry among the sheepfolds,
>   to hear the piping for the flocks?
> Among the clans of Reuben
>   there were great searchings of heart.
> Gilead stayed beyond the Jordan;
>   and Dan, why did he abide with the ships?
> Asher sat still at the coast of the sea,
>   settling down by his landings. (Judg. 5:14-17)

Their song celebrates the participation of the tribes of Ephraim, Benjamin, Zebulun, and Issachar, but laments the reticence of the tribes of Reuben and Dan and the clan of Gilead from the tribe of Manasseh to join the battle. Throughout this period, we find this tension between the sense of being a part of the covenanted congregation/assembly of "all Israel," and the daily reality of village life in households and clans.

With the appearance of the monarchy at the end of this period (roughly 1000 B.C.E.), the split between life as "Israel" and as local households and clans became even greater. Although most of the Hebrew Scriptures speak of "Israel" or "Judah" as if they were embodied characters with a collective voice, we must recognize that many biblical writers, especially those after exile, used this image in their attempt to restore people's (lost) sense of being part of something bigger than their local household/clan. It is fair to imagine that both during the monarchy and after the exile, most Israelites outside Jerusalem hardly thought of themselves as different in practical ways from the people around them. This, of course, was deemed by the biblical writers as a primary cause of God's angry punishment: the abandonment of the (Jerusalem-centered) covenant, which was intended to make them a holy people set apart from the ways of their neighbors of other "nations" (Hebrew *goyim*; Greek *ethnē*).

Living according to the ancient covenant became even more challenging for "Israelites" who found themselves living outside the land of Canaan after the exile. First in Babylon we hear the cry of the Psalmist: "How could we sing the Lord's song in a foreign land?" (Ps. 137:4). Later, in what is known as the Diaspora, Israelites found themselves settled for the long haul in "strange" lands such as Alexandria in Egypt. It was here that scribes realized that the Hebrew Scriptures needed to be translated into Greek or risk being rendered totally obsolete. Thus, in the third century before the common era, as the Greek empire swept the Mediterranean with its culture, the Septuagint was created in Alexandria. For the first time, people heard themselves described as the *ekklēsia* of God.

The Ekklēsiai *of Athens and of God*

For what was originally expressed in Hebrew does not have exactly the same sense when translated into another language. Not only this work, but even the law itself, the prophecies, and the rest of the books differ not a little as originally expressed. (*Prologue to Sirach*)

The book of Sirach is part of the collection of writings known as the deutero-canonical or "apocryphal" texts. It, like Baruch, the

Wisdom of Solomon, and other works, was composed in Hebrew but translated into Greek for "Israelites" living in the cities outside Canaan, primarily in Alexandria. As the quotation suggests, for people whose ancestors heard God's word in the sacred language of Hebrew, listening to or reading it in Greek was a new and different experience. Anyone who has been brought up with a sense of the Bible gained from the King James and has later heard it in a modern English translation such as the New American or New Revised Standard knows something of this experience. How much more so is it the case for people who, raised with the Bible in English, have picked up even a modicum of biblical Greek or Hebrew. The audience of the Septuagint were the first Bible hearers and readers to have this experience.

Translation is an art, not a science. Bilingual people know this as they search their minds for a word or phrase suitable to match one from another language. The Septuagint is not a word-for-word rendering of the Hebrew Scriptures into Greek. It is an act of interpretation. In some places, this interpretation meant simply trying to deal with differences between Greek and Hebrew grammar, wordplay, assonance, and so forth. In others, it meant actually changing or adding words to texts which the interpreters either didn't fully understand or thought they did but were embarrassed by them. Throughout, however, it meant using words that had developed in a cultural setting very different from that of biblical Hebrew.

One of the key instances of this translation difficulty was in rendering the Hebrew terms *qahal* and *ʿedah* into Greek. On purely linguistic grounds, it was not particularly troublesome. *Ekklēsia,* like *qahal,* designates what we would call in English an "assembly." The theological implications for being "church," then and now, derive from the cultural context from which the term *ekklēsia* was drawn.

For hundreds of years before Jesus and even for generations before the Septuagint, *ekklēsia* referred to the Hellenistic civic body called out from the general populace to make political decisions, something like the U.S. House of Representatives. However, in ancient Athens and other Greek city-states, a large portion of the male "citizenry" participated in this process. In numerical terms, this meant that of the approximately 250,000 total population of Athens at its peak, some 6,000 of the 30,000 adult male citizens took part. Of course, the downside of this democratic process, at least from a modern perspective, was not only the total exclusion of women but the foundation of male citizen "freedom" on the work of between eighty and one hundred thousand slaves. The adoption of this term to describe discipleship communities nearly five centuries later was both modeled on and diverged radically from this original Hellenistic context.

When applied to the ancient texts of Hebrew Scripture, the use of *ekklēsia* must have given, as Sirach suggests, a different ring to the sense of God's assembled people. Just as we can hardly hear the word "church" without thinking of buildings and historical institutions, a citizen of Alexandria or, later, other cities of the Greco-Roman world, could hardly hear *ekklēsia* without envisioning civic assemblies.

How would this Hellenistic, urban resonance have shaped their understanding of the ancestral assembly of Israel? It was probably not too different from what today's Christians unconsciously do when they refer, as I often have heard people do, to the "Jewish church" of biblical times. It is hard not to listen to ancient texts through one's own cultural context. What theological or practical difference might this cultural listening filter make to urban "Israelites'" perceptions of what they were called by God to be a part of? Consider, for instance, Deuteronomy's narrative of criteria for admission into the *ekklēsia*.

> Those born of an illicit union shall not be admitted to the assembly of the Lord (*ekklēsian kyriou*). Even to the tenth generation, none of their descendants shall be admitted to the assembly of the Lord.
> No Ammonite or Moabite shall be admitted to the assembly of the Lord. Even to the tenth generation, none of their

descendants shall be admitted to the assembly of the Lord. (Deut. 23:2-3)

Here the *ekklēsia* membership is bounded by ethnic criteria. Now consider a secular Greek text, in this case, from *The Politics* of Aristotle:*

> For the best material of democracy is an agricultural population; there is no difficulty in forming a democracy where the mass of the people live by agriculture or tending of cattle. Being poor, they have no leisure, and therefore do not often attend the assembly (*ekklēsia*), and not having the necessaries of life they are always at work, and do not covet the property of others. Indeed, they find their employment pleasanter than the cares of government or office where no great gains can be made out of them, for the many are more desirous of gain than of honor.

From a philosophical perspective, the criterion is class division. Poor farmers have no time, and thus, Aristotle presumes, no interest in "the cares of government or office" that bring more "honor" than "gain." The philosopher's elitism toward the people of the land is, of course, nothing new or unique to Hellenism. This same prejudice could be found among Jerusalem's priestly and scribal elite, whether during the period of restoration from exile (e.g., Neh. 5) or during the time of Jesus (e.g., John 7:49). The point for our purposes is that Israelites in Alexandria, in considering criteria for gathering together the *ekklēsia*, would hear *both* messages, that of Hebrew Scripture and that of Hellenistic "wisdom." It was one thing to resist the local customs and religion of the indigenous people of Canaan, something that the biblical narrative says was not done very completely. It was another to

---

*Interestingly, the final version of Deuteronomy, likely composed during or soon after the Babylonian Exile, was not much older than Aristotle's own text, although its story world projects back a thousand years before the time of its composition. Probably between one and two hundred years separate them.

resist the ways of the dominant culture *outside the land* which Israel considered its own. This was especially true for educated folks like Sirach, who, not surprisingly, found much to admire in the heritage of Hellenism, just as we continue to study and learn from the ancient Greek thinkers, poets, and playwrights today.

The book of Sirach, typical of what is generally referred to as biblical "wisdom literature," addresses issues of concern to Israelites living under the influence of the great philosophical systems of Persia, Greece, and eventually, Rome. It was written in the second century B.C.E., generations after the original Septuagint translation but still over two hundred years before *ekklēsia* was applied to the gathered followers of Jesus. In a typical passage, it reflects on the role of the scribe (like Sirach himself) in relation to other occupations:

> The wisdom of the scribe depends on the opportunity of leisure; and he who has little business may become wise. How can he become wise who handles the plow, and who glories in the shaft of a goad, who drives oxen and is occupied with their work, and whose talk is about bulls? . . . So too is every craftsman and master workman. . . . So too is the smith sitting by the anvil. . . . So too is the potter sitting at his work. . . . All these rely upon their hands, and each is skillful in his own work. Without them a city cannot be established, and men can neither sojourn nor live there. Yet they are not sought out for the council of the people, nor do they attain eminence in the public assembly (*ekklēsia*). They do not sit in the judge's seat, nor do they understand the sentence of judgment; they cannot expound discipline or judgment, and they are not found using proverbs. But they keep stable the fabric of the world, and their prayer is in the practice of their trade. On the other hand he who devotes himself to the study of the law of the Most High will seek out the wisdom of all the ancients, and will be concerned with prophecies; he will preserve the discourse of notable men and penetrate the subtleties of parables; he will seek

out the hidden meanings of proverbs and be at home with
the obscurities of parables. He will serve among great men
and appear before rulers; he will travel through the lands of
foreign nations, for he tests the good and the evil among
men. (Sir. 38:24-39:4)

How much of Sirach's "wisdom" is biblical and how much
from Aristotle and other Greek thinkers? Note how, like Aristotle,
Sirach assumes both the importance of manual laborers of various kinds and their absence from the *ekklēsia*. In contrast, the
scribe not only may be found within the *ekklēsia* but "will serve
among great men and before rulers." We can see, then, that for
Israel's elite living in the Diaspora among Greeks, the image of
ekklēsia had been, at least in part, transformed from the assembly
of "all Israel" to an urban body composed of the intellectual (and
economic) movers and shakers.

Of course, both *ekklēsia* and *synagōgē* as used in the Septuagint
referred not primarily to the Greek political assembly but to the
historically covenanted assembly of Israelites. Whatever reso-
nances of Hellenistic secular assemblies might ring in the ears of
Alexandrian Israelites, there was always also the sense of *ekklēsia*
or *synagōgē* as YHWH's chosen people. What did it mean to
embody God's *ekklēsia* while living in a foreign country amidst
other cultures? The Hebrew Scriptures prior to the wisdom literature did not address this question, other than in lament as heard
in Psalm 137 noted earlier. To "sing the Lord's song in a foreign
land" must have seemed a tragic oxymoron to the Psalmist, but to
Israelites residing in Alexandria or other Mediterranean cities for
the long haul, it was both a theological and a practical question of
great importance. Indeed, one of the central tasks of Israel's Diaspora thinkers and writers was determining which aspects of
covenant practice made sense when they were uprooted from
Canaan and which did not. For example, it was obvious that the
Torah provisions dealing with Temple sacrifices would not apply
to people in foreign cities. But would Israelite men still be
required to travel to Jerusalem for the three annual festivals as

mandated by Leviticus? Would circumcision still be required of all males? Eating only approved, "clean" foods? These and other questions were addressed by many whose writings have survived. Those writings reflect no consensus on virtually any of these questions, as John J. Collins has clearly shown in his book *Athens and Jerusalem*. Rather, opinions ranged from those advocating close-to-absolute continuity with literal covenant practice to those for whom being a faithful Israelite could be reduced to expressing trust in God the Creator, who was also being celebrated and worshiped under other names by Hellenistic neighbors. One might note a similar diversity of opinion not only on what it means to be Jewish today living in the United States but also on what it means to be Christian.

In Alexandria, the city about which we know most on this topic, Israelites lived in freedom and dignity for generations alongside their Gentile neighbors. In fact, the evidence suggests that, although they were influenced by the dominant culture in many ways, they lived more or less in separate neighborhoods. They did business with Gentiles, but then returned home to their familiar subculture. Again, we have seen this pattern both among Jews in Europe and among European and Latin American Catholic immigrants in the United States. As much as possible, people tried to live in a "both/and" religious/cultural milieu. They accepted much of the surrounding culture as not only tolerable but something to be emulated, while at the same time revering the customs and traditions of their ancestors. It was into this situation that people like Paul the Jew came, preaching the Good News of Jesus Christ, and establishing "churches" in Jesus' name.

The Church of God in Corinth, Ephesus, and Elsewhere

As we have seen, the Septuagint used both *synagōgē* and *ekklēsia* to refer to assemblies of children of Israel. The New Testament, however, is wholly consistent in using *synagōgē* to refer to Jewish gatherings (and sometimes the gathering place itself) and *ekklēsia* for gatherings of Jesus' followers. The Jewish historian Josephus, writing from his experience in Jerusalem in the late first century C.E., uses *synagōgē* to refer to Jewish religious gatherings in post-biblical times, but freely uses *ekklēsia*, following the Septuagint, when he is telling Israel's history. He also uses *ekklēsia* to refer to secular gatherings, both Jewish and Roman. Interestingly, his only mention of followers of Jesus of Nazareth refers to them as "the tribe of Christians so named from him, [who] are not extinct at this day" (*Antiquities of the Jews* 18.3.3).

Thus, it seems that, independent of Christian influence, Jewish writers had begun to refer to their own religious gatherings exclusively as *synagōgē*. But this did not necessarily require New Testament writers to use a different term to refer to Christian gatherings and communities, and it certainly did not require that the specific term *ekklēsia* be used. Why, then, did this become the primary way to describe the discipleship communities and their assemblies? What did this usage convey to members and to those outside, whether Jew or Gentile?

Historically speaking, the first reference to Jesus' disciples as an *ekklēsia* is in Paul's first letter to those gathered in the city of Thessalonica on the Aegean seacoast. We know almost nothing about how this community was started. The only bit of evidence is the story told in Acts 17 about Paul's and Silas's stop in Thessalonica, where, Luke reports, Paul went into "a synagogue of the Jews" and on three sabbath days attempted to prove from the Hebrew Scriptures that Jesus was the Messiah. Luke tells us simply that "some of them were persuaded and joined Paul and Silas, as did a great many of the devout Greeks and not a few of the leading women" (Acts 17:4), but says nothing further about the outcome of this evangelical encounter. The scene in Acts dissolves as Paul's opponents hire some local thugs to start trouble and some of the believers are dragged before the city authorities, charged with "acting contrary to the decrees [Greek *dogmata*] of Caesar, saying that there is another king named Jesus" (17:7). The officials let them go without trial, however, and Paul and Silas, who had remained hidden during the disturbance, were spirited out of town under cover of darkness.

It is apparently this group of believers to whom Paul writes some time later, most likely in the mid-50s. He addresses his letter (written along with Silvanus and Timothy) to "the church [*ekklēsia*] of the Thessalonians in God the Father and the Lord Jesus Christ" (1 Thess. 1:1). He obviously expects them to understand the title with which he addresses them, for there is no explanation provided. Almost all the letters which most scholars agree were written by Paul begin similarly when addressing a community, with the exception of Romans and Philippians:

To the churches of Galatia (Gal. 1:2)

To the church of God that is in Corinth, to those who are sanctified in Christ Jesus, called to be saints [Greek *hagioi*], together with all those who in every place call on the name of our Lord Jesus Christ, both their Lord and ours (1 Cor. 1:2)

To the church of God that is in Corinth, including all the saints throughout Achaia (2 Cor. 1:1)

To Philemon our dear friend and co-worker, to Apphia our sister, to Archippus our fellow soldier, and to the church in your house (Philm. 2)

Romans is addressed to "God's beloved in Rome, who are called to be saints" (Rom. 1:7) while Philippians is written to "all the saints in Christ Jesus who are in Philippi, with the overseers [Greek *episkopois*] and servants [Greek *diakonois*]" (Phil. 1:1). "Called to be saints," both in First Corinthians and in Romans, appears to refer to people considering or on the way to membership in the *ekklēsia*, while "saints" describes not particular holiness as in the modern sense of the term, but simply full membership in the *ekklēsia*.

Ephesians and Colossians, which many would attribute to a writer other than Paul, begin:

> To the saints and faithful brothers in Christ in Colossae (Col. 1:2)

> To the saints who are in Ephesus and are faithful in Christ Jesus (Eph. 1:1)

We can see that it was certainly Paul's consistent practice to refer to the discipleship communities as *ekklēsiai,* and to the persons themselves as "saints" or "brothers." We will look at the implications of these other terms later. Paul appears to be the initiator of this usage, for the Gospels virtually never tell of Jesus using the term *ekklēsia. It is clearly anachronistic to think of Jesus' "establishing" or even starting a "church" in his lifetime.* As far as we can tell, the ministry of Jesus involved traveling from place to place, preaching, healing, and casting out unclean spirits as he went, not "founding" communities. On his journeys, he is accompanied by people referred to as "disciples," "apostles," or the Twelve, along with the shifting crowds. The only Gospel passages that suggest otherwise are Matthew 16:18 and 18:15-21. In the first, Jesus says that Peter is the rock (Greek *petros*) upon which Jesus "will build my church." Matthew has Jesus speak of a future event which has not yet taken place. In the second passage, Jesus speaks of the need to develop a just and compassionate process for resolving disputes among "the brothers." He says that if disputes cannot be resolved among two or three, they should be brought before the *ekklēsia.* That Matthew has Jesus speak here of *ekklēsia* in the present tense having just previously had Jesus speak of the "building" of an *ekklēsia* as a future event shows that this is the *evangelist*'s understanding of the gospel, rather than Jesus' own words. No other Gospel reports such a statement, nor do they use *ekklēsia* at all. Matthew's Gospel, most likely written in the late first century, at least a generation after Paul's authentic letters, must therefore derive its use of *ekklēsia* not from Jesus but from Paul and others who carried the Good News to the cities of the Roman empire.

This makes sense precisely because of the differing contexts of Jesus and Paul: the villages and countryside of Galilee and Judea versus the urban centers of empire. As we will see, one of the central attractions of the *ekklēsiai* was the formation of bonds of fellowship and mutual security among otherwise alienated city dwellers. Village peasants and small-town people had long-established bonds with one another that had been disrupted by Roman oppression. When Jesus sought to lead these people to a renewed sense of being God's own people despite Roman claims, he appealed to memories not of *ekklēsia* but of Israel's wilderness and tribal confederations (e.g., Mark 6:34-44; cf. Luke 1:13-17; 2:28-35). Although Jesus was passionately concerned with leading rural, Palestinian Jews into a renewed sense of their historic, tribal interconnection under God's exclusive authority ("the reign of God"), the development of "church" was wholly an urban phenomenon, even in Palestine, where Luke speaks of the *ekklēsia* almost exclusively in Jerusalem.* Other New Testament writers follow this pattern. For example, we hear the author of First Peter say, "Your sister church in Babylon, chosen together with you, sends you greetings" (1 Pet. 5:13; see also Jas. 5:14; 3 John 1:6, 9). Most pointedly, John of Patmos, author of the book of Revelation, addresses his narrative to "the seven churches that are in Asia" (Rev. 1:4). Throughout his book, he exhorts these communities set in cities of the Roman province of Asia to live as people "called out" from the matrix of empire in which they find themselves, envisioned as the whore Babylon: "Come out of her, my

---

*The one exception is his statement in Acts 9:31: "the church throughout Judea, Galilee, and Samaria had peace and was built up." This isolated comment does not contradict the urban nature of the *ekklēsia*, however, but is part of Luke's larger program of portraying the Holy Spirit's empowering presence at Pentecost like a wind blowing Good News across the land.

people, so that you do not take part in her sins, and so that you do not share in her plagues" (Rev. 18:4).

From John's vision we can work backward to see that *ekklēsia* is used as a name for the urban discipleship communities precisely so that they can see themselves as people "called out" to live as God's assembly according to a Way entirely opposed to that of empire. For Jews who became convinced that Jesus was the Messiah, this meant a renewed commitment to live as God's chosen people. Hellenized Jews raised on the Septuagint (most of whom probably could not read or understand biblical Hebrew) would hear in *ekklēsia* the echo of God's calling out of Egypt a people destined to live outside of Egypt's orbit. Educated Gentiles who felt "called to be saints" would likely recognize in *ekklēsia* the "ancient" tradition of Greek democracy—over four hundred years old by Paul's day—from before the world was controlled by Greek or Roman imperial rule. Even Romans could hear the more recent memory of the preimperial Republic, when philosophical principles and reasoned debate were used to seek the common good. In the exhortations of Paul, John of Patmos and Luke as narrator of Acts, people from all the urban traditions of the Mediterranean could hear a call to become a "community of the called out," a new society grounded not in dominating political power nor even in philosophical wisdom, but in the Word of God revealed in Jesus and the Hebrew Scriptures. Its pledge of allegiance was stated in terms unequivocal in their commitment: "Jesus Christ is Lord" (Phil. 2:11), "this is truly the Savior of the world" (John 4:42), "My Lord and my God" (John 20:28), and so forth. These statements were battle cries in a spiritual war: Jesus and his God were the ones from whom true power flowed, to whom people should turn in trust and thanksgiving, and *not* Caesar or other human rulers. As Matthew's Jesus says, "Call no one your father on earth, for you have one Father, the one in heaven" (Matt. 23:9; cf. John 1:12-13).

Such confessions were not only unequivocal; they were politically subversive. Just as Rome's representative in Judea, Pontius

Pilate, is portrayed challenging Jesus and the Judean leaders on their loyalties to the emperor (e.g., John 18:36-39; 19:12-15), Paul and company are shown to be challenged by their hearers. In Thessalonica, as we heard above, Luke says they were accused of acting against the *dogmata* of Caesar and proclaiming "another king named Jesus." Similarly, in the Roman colony of Philippi, a woman shouts that they "proclaim to you a way of salvation," which leads to the charge of "advocating customs that are not lawful for us as Romans to adopt or observe" (Acts 16:17, 21). Lost to our modern ears is the fact that "salvation" (Greek *sôtêria*) was the bailiwick of the emperor. To proclaim Jesus Lord, Savior, or King was to reject the authority of empire in one's life and therefore to risk serious consequences.

It is one thing to say within a closed-door gathering or in one's own heart, "Jesus is Lord," and quite another to live according to that confession in one's daily, publicly observable life. Calling the discipleship community an *ekklēsia* meant that members were not simply to "go to church" once a week and get a battery charge for the daily grind of imperial life. Rather, they were to see their primary loyalty, their primary identity, as members of a new society, living within, but not according to, the ways of "the world" (e.g., John 14:17-21; 16:8-11; 17:13-18).

But what did this mean in daily life? How was and is one to live within an imperial context while maintaining one's practical trust in the God of Jesus? How was one to have joy and live as loving people in a world filled with exploitation, injustice, and so much unnecessary suffering? This was the primary question facing the *ekklēsia*, the one which will take up the remainder of this book.

Reflection Questions

1. What associations do you have with the term "church"? What are the sources for these associations: for example, family, teachers, pastors or other church authorities, or others? How do

the images of church in this chapter challenge or reinforce those associations?

2. Ancient Israelites, along with the first followers of Jesus, found themselves attempting to be faithful to God amidst a series of empires. Would you describe your own social, political, and economic context as "imperial"? Why or why not? If so, what are the implications of this imperial context for your own sense of being church?

3. Consider a faith community of which you are a part or of which you are aware. What would it mean to imagine this community as being "called out" from the wider cultural milieu? Consider features of church life that express either continuity with or discontinuity from the surrounding culture(s). What traditions are used either to reinforce or deny a sense of being "called out"?

2

Singing a New Song

Prayer and Worship in the Ekklēsia

For most Christians today, Sunday worship is the central if not the only regular occasion for being part of "church." It may be surprising to discover, therefore, that the New Testament rarely speaks about the *ekklēsia* gathered for prayer and liturgy. In the Gospels, Jesus goes off by himself or with a few friends to pray. He responds to the disciples' request for a specific "Jesus prayer" by teaching them what became known as the Our Father or the Lord's Prayer. He counsels his frustrated and embarrassed disciples who found their power to exorcise an evil spirit lacking that "this kind can come out only through prayer" (Mark 9:29). But with the exception of the celebration at the Last Supper, we almost never find Jesus gathered with his friends outside the synagogue context for anything we might call "liturgy."

Paul taught the *ekklēsia* in Corinth how to conduct their eucharistic assemblies in accordance with the Spirit's guidance and frequently spoke of his own prayer and that of his audiences for one another's needs and support, as do other epistle writers. Only the book of Revelation portrays communal celebration of worship in its seven scenes of "heavenly liturgy." To understand the practice and ideals of the early *ekklēsia*, then, we must look carefully at the texts that speak to these basic questions. We will consider in this chapter the following aspects of the *ekklēsia*'s activities:

1. Communal celebration of God and Jesus
2. Communal prayer for mutual well-being and strength
3. The practice of baptism
4. Remembrance of Jesus in a communal meal
5. Footwashing
6. Forgiveness of sins/debts
7. Individual prayer
8. Communal discernment of spirits
9. Bible study

Communal Celebration of God and Jesus

It may seem obvious, but we must start from the recognition that Jesus did not "say mass" or offer sacraments as we have come to know them. As a Jew, he had been raised with a consciousness of the traditions of Moses contained within the Torah and as taught by lay people such as the Pharisees. Yet he was openly critical of the hypocrisy of the Jerusalem Temple's priestly establishment and others who manipulated Torah proscriptions to serve their own ends. Furthermore, Jesus was highly selective in the traditional worship practices he saw as continuing to serve his understanding of the divine will. Any practice that supported and inspired people's commitment to trust in God alone would have been seen as good and holy. Others he rejected, such as the idea that forgiveness could be granted only by formal priestly procedures (e.g., Mark 11:25; John 20:23). He also led people away from the tradition that the Jerusalem Temple and its festivals were central to attainment of holiness, teaching people to worship together as their ancestors had: in the wilderness, on mountains, and in communal gatherings in homes.

According to the Gospels, Jesus' followers were extremely confused about whose wisdom to listen to regarding prayer and worship. All external evidence told them that the Jerusalem priests and scribes were the most holy of people. They presided over rituals enshrouded in tradition and every kind of visible pomp, from fancy clothes to extravagant displays of incense and gold. Yet, as people who came to Jesus looking for some sign that God was at work in their midst, they must have wondered why those deemed holiest seemed aligned with the imperial powers that taxed the people into desperation. They must have wondered, too, why the God who drew a band of slaves out of Egypt seemed so unconcerned with the price demanded of the poor to achieve righteousness, at least according to the bearers of the official tradition. Jesus responded regularly to these confusions by publicly humiliating the priests and scribes, in order to break the hypnotic hold their visible power had on many people. For instance, in Mark's Gospel, Jesus tells his Jerusalem crowd,

> Beware of the scribes, who like to walk around in long robes, and to be greeted with respect in the marketplaces, and to have the best seats in the synagogues and places of honor at banquets! They devour widows' houses and for the sake of appearance say long prayers. They will receive the greater condemnation. (Mark 12:38-40)

In Matthew's Gospel, Jesus issues a harsh tirade that goes on for over twenty verses—extremely long by the standards of biblical narrative—against the Jerusalem scribes and Pharisees, calling them "hypocrites," "blind guides," "whitewashed tombs," and a "brood of vipers" (Matt. 23:15-36). This is incredibly strong language to direct at those considered by most folk to be paragons of virtue and holiness! Yet it is preceded by Jesus' admonition to the crowd and disciples to "do whatever they teach you and follow it; but do not do as they do, for they do not practice what they teach" (23:3). He thus clearly distinguishes between the bad practice of the leaders and the tradition they represent because "the scribes and the Pharisees sit on Moses' seat" (23:2).

Thus, one reason we see so little description of, or discussion by Jesus of, specific, new worship and prayer practices is his basic understanding that people should be following the ways given by God through Moses. But what about after the first Easter? Didn't Jesus' rising imply new occasions and forms of prayerful celebration?

In Acts, Luke tells of the earliest days of the *ekklēsia* in Jerusalem, during which members participated in both Temple rituals and "the breaking of the bread and the prayers" (Acts 2:42, 47). It is not until the gospel had moved far beyond Jerusalem and Gentiles had become part of the *ekklēsia* that specifically Jesus-centered forms of worship were practiced apart from Jewish traditions. The heated debate over whether Gentile men had to be circumcised in order to become part of the *ekklēsia* (e.g., Acts 15; Rom. 2:25ff; Gal. 5:2-13) was only one aspect of the struggle over whether proclaiming Jesus as Lord made a person a member of a new religion separate from Judaism.

We see this tension between Jewish worship traditions and the proclamation of faith in Jesus portrayed most explicitly in Revelation's scenes of heavenly liturgy. John's descriptions of his visions reveal worship as it takes place "behind the veil," that is, in the time and place where God lives and reigns at the heart of the *ekklēsia*. Although the nominal location of these scenes is God's throne in "the sky," a close look at Revelation's apocalyptic imagery shows us that John is trying to tell his audience that what he sees taking place day and night "in heaven" is what is *supposed to be taking place right where they live*, in the *ekklēsiai* of Ephesus, Pergamum, Smyrna, and so forth. "Heaven," in other words, is not a place in the sky or at the end of time, but the context in which the *ekklēsia* is intended to live its daily life, right on the streets of empire. The churches are to join their worship with the worship that is always taking place on "the other side."

What, according to John's vision, does heavenly liturgy look and sound like? For one thing, it is frequently *loud*. Great, thunderous waves of singing and cheering sweep across the liturgical scene like the shouts of football fans celebrating a last-minute victory touchdown. Consider just one of these images:

> Then I looked, and I heard the voice of many angels surrounding the throne and the living creatures and the elders; they numbered myriads of myriads and thousands of thousands, singing with a great voice, "Worthy is the Lamb that was slaughtered to receive power and wealth and wisdom and might and honor and glory and blessing!" Then I heard every creature in heaven and on earth and under the earth and in the sea, and all that is in them, singing, "To the one seated on the throne and to the Lamb be blessing and honor and glory and might forever and ever!" And the four living creatures said, "Amen!" And the elders fell down and worshiped. (Rev. 5:11-14)

Contained within this one passage is the essence of Revelation's theology of worship. First, the *ekklēsia* is not alone when it comes together in praise and thanksgiving, but is always accompanied by the countless angels and others who make up God's entourage. To appreciate the power of this statement, we must stop to gain some perspective on the quantitative relationship between the *ekklēsia* and its surrounding society. In Ephesus, for example, various estimates put the first-century population at roughly 200,000. While this is not a big city by today's standards, this population was densely packed into a small, walled area, which would have made the feeling of crowding as intense as in one of today's urban cores. Of these, perhaps as many as a hundred or as few as twenty persons would have been part of Revelation's Ephesian audience. As a tiny and distrusted minority, then, the sense of being accompanied by myriads of angels would have offered great comfort, strength, and solidarity.

The song sung by the angels and elders is a pull-out-all-the-stops praise of Jesus, the Lamb that was slaughtered and yet lives. It proclaims that he is the fitting recipient of seven attributes.

Individually and collectively, these attributes announce that Jesus—and not Caesar, the goddess Artemis, or other local gods and goddesses—is the proper object of worship and praise. The language, although joyous and celebratory, is blatantly political and subversive of empire. It is as if a Sunday hymn in an American church cried out, "we pledge allegiance to Jesus!" Non-Christian neighbors hearing such lyrics ringing through the church walls would rightly be suspicious of worshipers' loyalties to the nation and its leaders. This was precisely the point: to inculcate a deep sense of the salvific necessity of giving one's commitment to Jesus and his God alone.

The central reason Jesus is deemed worthy of such high praise is his "conquest" of empire through his victorious death and resurrection (Rev. 5:5). For people engaged in a literal, daily, life-and-death struggle with empire—whether as active resisters or simply in trying to survive—Jesus' resurrection is the best possible news: God is truly more powerful than Caesar and has proven it by raising Jesus from the dead to share forever in God's heavenly reign. Jesus' fidelity to and through the pathway of death has "redeemed" people from every tribe, tongue, people, and nation, freeing them from their debt to empire. It is exultation in this amazing, empowering, liberating event that causes the multitude to break out in their songs and shouts of celebration.

John's vision of worship continues by showing that the *ekklēsia* is joined in its song not only by angels but by *all of creation*. The birds and trees know nothing of allegiance to empire, but only to their Creator. Their very existence is a celebration, a point Jesus himself made, in contrasting the glory of the lilies of the field with the imperial regalia of Solomon (Matt. 6:28-29). Worship, according to Revelation, is intended to remove the blinders put over our eyes by empire, which convince us falsely that we owe thanksgiving and honor to it rather than to God alone. When we sing God's praises with full hearts and voices, we are simply joining in the song that takes place "24/7" in the world "behind the veil."

Revelation's narrative shows other forms of worship in addition to singing. Worshipers burn incense in golden bowls, prostrate themselves before the throne on which God and the Lamb are seated, wave palm branches, blow trumpets and strum kitharas (a lutelike instrument, often misleadingly translated as "harps") and generally have a grand old time celebrating the victory of the Lamb over the Beast of empire. The call to worship is, "Let us rejoice and exult and give God glory!" (Rev. 19:7). Far from somber or boring occasions, the scenes of heavenly liturgy remind the *ekklēsia* that proclaiming one's loyalty to God and God's Lamb is the greatest possible reason for turning up the volume and letting the good times roll.

Back on the ground, though, we find Paul struggling with the *ekklēsia* in Corinth as their joyous enthusiasm boils over into noisy confusion (1 Cor. 14). Word has reached him that their worship has become a cacophony of prophecies, singing, teaching, and speaking in tongues. These gifts are being abused, as is the occasion of the Lord's Supper, to show off the greatness of individuals. Paul urges an order of worship oriented toward a single goal: "that the *ekklēsia* may be built up" (1 Cor. 14:5). What is the value, he maintains, of displaying gifts of the Spirit, if no one has a clue what is being said because all are talking at once?

It is in this context that Paul's famously misunderstood statement about women's silence in church is made.* After making clear that disharmonious worship neither truly praises God nor edifies those considering joining the *ekklēsia*, Paul offers a few basic guidelines for establishing order. First, he says, "If anyone speaks in a tongue, let there be only two or at most three, and each in turn; and let one interpret" (1 Cor. 14:27). In this way, each Spirit-gift can be received and enjoyed by all. Then he continues, "But if there is no one to interpret, let them be silent in *ekklēsia* and speak to themselves and to God" (1 Cor. 14:28). The point is simply that the uninterpreted tongue is of no value to those who cannot understand what is being proclaimed. Silence, therefore, is better than a useless display. Second, he applies a similar rule for those who have been given a prophecy: "Let two or three prophets

---

*Although some scholars argue, with good reason, that these verses are not from Paul but are a later interpolation, they are shaped to fit the wider context of this section of First Corinthians and are understood by most readers as part of the canonical text.

speak, and let the others discern what is said." Finally, he speaks of women's silence. We cannot examine this controversial passage in depth here, but two points must be made to understand Paul's purpose. First, he is not issuing a blanket prohibition against women's voices in *ekklēsia*. Earlier he spoke of "any woman who prays or prophesies" in the context of the relationship between men and women in the broader context of church (1 Cor. 11:5), a topic we will take up in chapters 3 and 4. For now, simply notice that Paul takes for granted that women are part of the praying and prophesying community. Second, his central concern in 1 Corinthians 14 is establishing rules of order that generate worship that builds up the *ekklēsia,* not establishing blanket rules about liturgy and gender. Many have speculated about the specific concern that Paul is addressing in 14:33-36. Some have plausibly argued that it is a matter of practice parallel to the Delphic oracle, a very popular setting for women's loud proclamations and questioning (cf. Acts 16:16-19, where Paul exorcises a "pythonic spirit" from a slave girl in Philippi who is being used by her "owners" as a source of great profit via her fortune-telling). Unfortunately, neither First Corinthians nor any other of Paul's letters offers any insight on this question. Perhaps it will suffice to say that the issue never comes up in other letters, nor does any other New Testament writer purport to ban women from the pulpit or other places in worship services.

In sum, we see that while Jesus himself established no specific forms of "Christian" liturgy, his followers understood that their coming together was an occasion in which joyous celebration oriented around building up the *ekklēsia* for ministry and mission was of the highest value.

Communal Prayer for Mutual Wellbeing and Strength

As Revelation portrays the *ekklēsia*'s prayer joining in a "vertical" communion with the heavenly liturgy, many urban New

Testament writers make clear that the community's prayer also has a "horizontal" power. That is, each *ekklēsia* not only offers its own thanksgiving and praise to God but also prays for one another. There is no doubt that the early *ekklēsiai* thought that their prayerful remembrance of one another was a meaningful and effective act. For example, we hear James's advice:

> Are any among you suffering? They should pray. Are any cheerful? They should sing songs of praise. Are any among you sick? They should call for the elders of the church and have them pray over them, anointing them with oil in the name of the Lord. The prayer of faith will save the sick, and the Lord will raise them up; and anyone who has committed sins will be forgiven. Therefore confess your sins to one another, and pray for one another, so that you may be healed. The prayer of the righteous is powerful and effective. (Jas. 5:13-16)

We see this faith in the practical power of communal prayer dramatized in Acts, where more than once the *ekklēsia* pray for those in dire circumstances and see results (e.g., Acts 12:5-17; 16:25-26). This trust is in continuity with Israel's tradition, expressed most powerfully in the Psalms, that God truly hears and responds to the prayers of God's people in need.

At other times, the community prays for other communities with whom they have only spiritual contact because of the barrier of geographic distance. Paul regularly insists on the necessity and value of such prayer. For example,

> We always give thanks to God for all of you and mention you in our prayers, constantly. (1 Thess. 1:2)

> We always pray for you, asking that our God will make you worthy of his call and will fulfill by his power every good resolve and work of faith. (2 Thess. 1:11)

> Devote yourselves to prayer, keeping alert in it with thanksgiving. At the same time pray for us as well that God will

open to us a door for the word, that we may declare the mystery of Christ, for which I am in prison, so that I may reveal it clearly, as I should. (Col. 4:2)

As we will see in chapter 3 below, this spiritual practice is part of the *ekklēsia*'s sense of being part of a worldwide network of discipleship communities mutually responsible for one another, not unlike ancient Israel's sense of tribal interdependence. As they are to support one another in the challenging call to live social and economic relationships as much as possible outside the control of empire, so they are to pray for another to maintain the spiritual strength necessary to trust in God alone.

Such mutuality in prayer among the *ekklēsiai* is not an occasional act like Sunday worship, but a *constant* communion of hearts and minds. We see in Paul's words to the Thessalonians quoted above his commitment to pray "constantly" and "always," a theme that resounds throughout his writings and those in his name (e.g., Rom. 1:9; Phil. 1:4; Eph. 1:16-17; 6:18-19; 2 Tim. 1:3). Obviously, such prayer is a matter not of incessant recitation of words but of an effort to remain perpetually open to the Spirit who animates all the *ekklēsiai*. Just as individuals in a household support one another through the inevitable waves of clarity and confusion, joy and depression, hope and despair that characterize the human spiritual journey, so the churches are to provide support for one another for the long haul.

Paul certainly understood that such commitment requires spiritual discipline and practice. In a world where prayer was often seen as the province of official cult leaders such as imperial and Jerusalem priests, many ordinary folks might not have felt empowered to address God with prayer. We will see below Jesus' response to this in his provision of what we call the Lord's Prayer. For Paul, it meant a trust that the sheer desire to be in communion with God and one's fellow discipleship communities was a powerful force in itself. As he said to the Roman *ekklēsia*,

... the Spirit helps us in our weakness; for we do not know how to pray as we ought, but that very Spirit intercedes with groanings too deep for words. And God, who searches the heart, knows what is the mind of the Spirit, because the Spirit intercedes for the saints according to the will of God. (Rom. 8:26-27)

Paul thus reminds the *ekklēsia* that the effectiveness of prayer on behalf of others is not dependent on the quality or quantity of human effort, but is an expression of God's constant care and oversight of God's people. The *ekklēsiai* are to pray for one another not to arouse an otherwise inattentive deity to action but to align themselves with the power of the Spirit already at work, day and night, leading them on the Way.

Baptism

One of the biggest differences between traditional Israelite religious practice and that of the *ekklēsia* was the latter's enormous energy expended on adding new members. We will look in chapter 5 at how evangelization fit into the *ekklēsia*'s sense of mission. For now, we will focus on what the *ekklēsia* did to mark people's admission into the community. There is no doubt that the central ritual of initiation was baptism.

We start by recognizing that Jesus himself never baptized (e.g., John 4:2). Only in Matthew does Jesus expressly command his disciples to baptize others (Matt. 28:19). Curiously, the New Testament never tells of the apostles or the disciples who knew Jesus in the flesh being baptized themselves. Finally, although many New Testament texts speak of baptism as the primary ritual and mark of church membership, only Acts specifies that this involved water (Acts 8:36-39; 10:47-48; cf. John 9:7). To understand the importance of this ritual as a dividing line between an old life and a new one, we must compare it briefly with what we know of the baptismal traditions that preceded it.

The Greek verbs *baptō* and *baptizō* have the primary meanings respectively of "to dip" and "to wash." Both Greek words, like their

English counterparts, had application in the ordinary contexts of daily life. In the Septuagint, *baptō* is used nineteen times, almost always in the context of religious ritual. The most common usage is to refer to the priest's dipping his finger in animal blood or oil to purify the altar or some other object (e.g., Lev. 4:6; 14:16). It is used for dipping in water an object that had been made ritually unclean by contact with a dead and unclean animal, in order ritually to purify the object (Lev. 11:32). It is never used for putting water on a person.

Baptizō is found only four times in the Septuagint, once metaphorically (Isa. 21:4) and three times for human bathing in water (e.g., Jdt. 12:7). Sirach, in pleading for true conversion of heart from sin to God's way, laments rhetorically, "If one washes [Greek *baptizomenos*] after touching a dead body, and touches it again, what has one gained by washing [Greek *loutrō*]?" (Sir. 34:25). Most importantly for our purpose, we hear in 2 Kings 5 the story of Naaman, the Aramean army commander, who is told that the prophet Elisha can cure his skin disease. It is a wonderful story, in which the foreign commander resists when Elisha tells him, "Go, wash [Greek *lousai*] in the Jordan seven times, and your flesh shall be restored and you shall be clean." Naaman petulantly complains, "'I thought that for me he would surely come out, and stand and call on the name of YHWH his God, and would wave his hand over the spot, and cure the disease! Are not Abana and Pharpar, the rivers of Damascus, better than all the waters of Israel? Could I not wash in them, and be clean?' He turned and went away in a rage" (2 Kgs. 5:11-12). But Naaman's servants convince him to give up his nationalistic pride, and he obeys. The text then says, "So he went down and immersed himself [Greek *ebaptisato*] seven times in the Jordan, according to the word of the man of God; his flesh was restored like the flesh of a young boy, and he was clean" (2 Kgs. 5:14). He then returns to Elisha, offering a present to the prophet and praise to YHWH.

Surely this story was known both to John the Baptist and to Luke, who tells a similar story of Jesus' encounter in Samaria with ten people with skin diseases (Luke 17:12-19). The Baptist takes the tradition of the prophetic healing of a foreigner via immersion in the Jordan River, blends it with the Torah tradition of priestly purification through sprinkling of fluids and dipping in water, and, reading the signs of his times, begins a ministry of baptism for *metanoia*. This noun—usually translated "repentance"—and its cognate verb, *metanoeō*, mean literally "a different mind" and "to change one's mind." John's baptism was focused not on an intellectual conversion as, say, a move from one philosophical school to another, but on a complete transformation of one's thoughts, behavior, and social relationships. Thus, when the people reported in Luke's Gospel to have come to be baptized ask what they must do to "bear fruit worthy of *metanoia*," John's response is totally in economic terms (Luke 3:7-14). When Jesus begins his public ministry, he marks it by being baptized into John's sense of *metanoia* (Mark 1:9; Matt. 3:13-15; Luke 3:21; cf. John 1:29-34).

Thus we can see that Jesus, like John, thought that God's work was to bring people immersed in imperial lies and religious hypocrisy into a new way of life, entrance into which was symbolized by baptism. It is important to note that while John baptized in water, he made a point of distinguishing Jesus' baptism as one "in the Holy Spirit" (Mark 1:8; Acts 1:5) or "in Holy Spirit and fire" (Matt. 3:11; Luke 3:16). It is into this experience that the apostles and other disciples are immersed (Acts 1:8; 2:1-4). To be "baptized" in the Holy Spirit, then, is to be "possessed" by God's own personality, to allow one's words and actions to reveal God's ways to others.

Paul speaks frequently of the importance of baptism, although never of how it is to be done. He is concerned less with the formalities of water and ritual procedures than with the meaning of the act of commitment that baptism signifies. It is a form of *dying* which treats one's previous way of life as buried (Rom. 6:3-4; cf. Col. 2:12). The result of this process is to be "clothed" with Christ, a reality in which the central distinctions through which the world generates power of some over others are abolished (Gal. 3:27-28). Similarly, the author of First Peter says that Noah's salvation from the Flood via the ark "prefigured" baptism, "not as a removal of dirt from the body, but as an appeal to God for a good conscience, through the resurrection of Jesus Christ" (1 Pet. 3:21). Throughout Acts, we see baptism as the first step taken by those who accept the gospel preached by the apostles and who join the *ekklēsia* (Acts 2:41; 8:12, 38; 9:18; 10:48; 16:15, 33; 18:8; 19:5). These passages together point to the central importance of baptism, however performed, as the mark of exit from the sinful, imperial world and of entry into a community that knew itself as "the called out."

Knowing Jesus in the Breaking of the Bread

Today's ordinary Catholic mass or mainline Protestant communion service bears little resemblance to what we can glean from the New Testament about the first celebrations of Jesus' presence in the breaking of the bread. Arguments that have divided denominations over the question of the relationship between the blessed bread and the whereabouts of Jesus would certainly have seemed strange and irrelevant to the first *ekklēsiai*. The New Testament speaks simply, both in the Gospels and in other writings, of memory and presence, without theological elaboration. Because of our modern historical obsession with what one might call "left-brain" (rational) inquiries about a "right-brain" (affective) experience, we have often lost the essence of what Jesus intended and Paul understood about Eucharist.

In the ancient world, as in virtually every culture throughout history, people celebrated their thankfulness for life and for one another through shared meals. Countless gods and goddesses have been worshiped, stories recalled, and relationships strengthened across the dinner table. For biblical Israel, this took many forms, including annual clan sacrificial celebrations that renewed transhousehold bonds (e.g., 1 Sam. 20:5-6). One of the central occasions for this experience was the annual celebration of Passover. Although the Torah links the origins of this feast to the historical Exodus from Egypt (Exod. 12), Hebrew Scripture recounts that at the time of King Josiah shortly before the Babylonian Exile,

> No such passover had been kept since the days of the judges who judged Israel, or during all the days of the kings of Israel or of the kings of Judah, but in the eighteenth year of King Josiah this passover was kept to YHWH in Jerusalem. (2 Kgs. 23:22-23)

Josiah's celebration of the Passover was part of his wider reform package which attempted to restore the people to their covenant relationship with YHWH alone, after centuries of assimilation to Canaanite religious and cultural practice. How could it be that what has been for nearly three millennia now the central Jewish feast was not practiced for the hundreds of years from the Exodus until just before the exile? If the report in Second Kings is historically accurate, it suggests that soon after settling into the Land, the Israelites abandoned the central memorial of their liberation by YHWH and their establishment as a covenant people. There are no obvious answers to this question. Some scholars have suggested that the festival itself was part of Josiah's reform, and its accompanying story was retrojected back into the Torah to give the feast legitimacy nearly six hundred years later. Others have argued that Passover had become a household and clan-based feast in resistance to the Jerusalem-centered demands of people such as Josiah and the Judean priesthood. Whatever the historical facts may be, by the time of Jesus, Passover was well established as the most important occasion of the year, replacing Tabernacles (*Sukkoth*), which had previously been the central feast. According to Deuteronomy—likely written by people supportive of Josiah's perspective—it was not to be offered "within any of your towns that YHWH your God is giving you, but at the place that YHWH your God will choose as a dwelling for his name [i.e., Jerusalem], only there shall you offer the passover sacrifice" (Deut. 16:5-6).

Thus, we find the Gospels consistently narrating the story of Jesus and his disciples journeying to Jerusalem for the Passover, although John's Gospel retains the tradition of Jesus' feeding a large crowd gathered for a *wilderness* Passover in subversive memory of the original Exodus liberation locale (John 6:3-14). In the Synoptic tradition, Jesus and his disciples celebrate the feast in an unidentified place, presumably the home of a Jerusalem disciple. The Gospels shroud the finding of this place in mystery and intrigue: two disciples are to go into the city and look for a man carrying a water jar, the equivalent of the spy-movie "man with a red carnation." They are given a special code phrase with which to identify themselves to the owner of the house. It is at this Passover meal that Jesus acts and speaks about eating bread in his memory. Because so much has been made of the precise meaning of Eucharist, it is worth comparing the three Synoptic accounts, which differ in substantial ways. Assuming with most scholars that Mark's account is the earliest of the three, I have highlighted in bold the words added by Matthew or Luke, while italicizing the portion of Mark omitted by the others.

> While they were eating, he took a loaf of bread, and after blessing it he broke it, gave it to them, and said, "Take; this is my body." Then he took a cup, and after giving thanks he gave it to them, *and all of them drank from it.* He said to them, "This is my blood of the covenant, which is poured out for many." (Mark 14:22-24)

> While they were eating, Jesus took a loaf of bread, and after blessing it he broke it, gave it to the disciples, and said, "Take, **eat**; this is my body." Then he took a cup, and after giving thanks [Greek *eucharistēsas*] he gave it to them, saying, "**Drink from it, all of you**; for this is my blood of the covenant, which is poured out for many **for the forgiveness of sins**." (Matt. 26:26-28)

> Then he took a loaf of bread, **and when he had given thanks**, he broke it and gave it to them, saying, "This is my body,

which is given for you. Do this in remembrance of me." And
he did the same with the cup **after supper,** saying, "This cup
that is poured out **for you is the new covenant in my
blood.**" (Luke 22:19-20)

Paul's account of this event is most likely the earliest of all. He
says,

> For I received from the Lord what I also handed on to you,
> that the Lord Jesus on the night when he was betrayed took
> a loaf of bread, and when he had given thanks, he broke it
> and said, "This is my body that is for you. Do this in remem-
> brance of me." In the same way he took the cup also, after
> supper, saying, "This cup is the new covenant in my blood.
> Do this, as often as you drink it, in remembrance of me." For
> as often as you eat this bread and drink the cup, you pro-
> claim the Lord's death until he comes. (1 Cor. 11:23-26)

Paul's version is most similar to Luke's, one factor among many
that suggest a historical link between these two writers. Note that
Paul expressly tells the *ekklēsia* in Corinth that he is passing on
what he "received from the Lord." Nowhere in Acts or Paul's letters does he say when or how he claims to have received this word
directly from the risen Jesus. But given that Paul carefully distinguishes in many places what he believes to be God's word from his
own advice, we must take seriously his statement that he is simply
transmitting established tradition.

Needless to say, more questions are raised by these passages
than can be addressed here. For instance, from Mark's or
Matthew's Gospel, one would not understand Jesus to be making
a statement addressed to anyone beyond the specific persons
gathered for the meal at which he sits. Mark's narrative implies a
one-time event. Luke and Paul go beyond that to suggest Jesus
calling for the ongoing performance of a memorial meal. Clearly,
that Paul is addressing the question of eucharistic practice in
Corinth at all makes certain that the *ekklēsia* understood Jesus to

have instructed them to establish such a memorial meal associated with the Jewish feast of Passover, and hence, to be understood as a celebration of a divine act of liberation from empire.
However, a major difference was that the eucharistic celebration,
also known as the Lord's Supper (1 Cor. 11:20), was to be practiced regularly rather than once a year. How often? Nothing in the
New Testament answers this question. Who is to lead it? Again,
there is silence.

What we do know, is that it was not a worship service with a
piece of bread symbolic of a meal, but an actual *feast*. Apart from
the specific "institution" passages cited, we have other narratives
that suggest the nature of what was to take place. For example,
Luke's Gospel ends with the wonderful story of the two disciples
meeting Jesus on the road to Emmaus, a scene we will revisit later
in this chapter. After walking with them, Jesus eventually joins
them for an evening meal. Luke tells,

> When he was at the table with them, he took bread, blessed
> and broke it, and gave it to them. Then their eyes were
> opened, and they recognized him; and he vanished from
> their sight. (Luke 24:30-31)

After the seven-mile journey from Jerusalem, what is envisioned here is not a mere bite, but a nourishing, satisfying meal.
And this is precisely the point of the early practice of Eucharist:
when one is thankful to God for the gift of life that is bread—the
combined fruit of the earth and work of human hands—remember Jesus! Note that when the disciples return from Emmaus to
Jerusalem, they proclaim not that Jesus *was* the bread, but that "he
had been made known to them in the breaking of the bread"
(Luke 24:35).

Similarly, although the tradition known by Paul, like the Synoptic Last Supper tradition, reports Jesus saying that the bread *is*
his body, Paul's emphasis in his letter is on the proclamation that
accompanies the act, rather than the nature of the bread itself.
When you do this, he says, you are proclaiming "the Lord's death

until he comes." Therefore, he counsels them, do not make the gathering simply another occasion for parading one's status according to worldly standards, which serves only to humiliate your sisters and brothers of less material wealth. Rather, acknowledge that when you share in this memorial meal, you are identifying with Jesus' death, a death that means for you a total abandonment of the "wisdom of the world" in favor of the wisdom of God, that is, the cross (e.g., 1 Cor. 1:17-31). If your eucharistic banquets do not serve to bring you in touch with this reality, Paul says, they are of no use at all, bringing judgment rather than grace (1 Cor. 11:28-29).

The only other New Testament text that deals with the question of the *ekklēsia*'s gathering for Eucharist is Jesus' so-called Bread of Life discourse in John's Gospel (John 6). In John's narrative, the Last Supper is the occasion on which Jesus speaks not of bread and wine but of footwashing, which we will examine later in this chapter. The Gospel's author certainly must have known, as Paul did probably thirty years or more earlier, that the Last Supper had been long associated with the memorial meal in Jesus' name. However, he displaces the conversation about bread to the earlier occasion of the Passover wilderness feeding, in which thousands apparently bereft of bread eat and are satisfied. The excited crowds attempt to corral Jesus into being the revolutionary Messiah king they are seeking, but he escapes from them across the sea of Galilee. When they finally catch up to him, they get caught up in a rabbinic discussion with him over the meaning of the Exodus passage about the manna as "bread from heaven" (Exod. 16). When he claims to *be* that bread, they resist, which leads Jesus to raise the rhetorical and theological stakes considerably:

> I am the living bread that came down from heaven. Whoever eats of this bread will live forever; and the bread that I will give for the life of the world is my flesh. . . . Very truly, I tell you, unless you eat the flesh of the Son of Man and drink his blood, you have no life in you. Those who munch my flesh and drink my blood have eternal life, and I will raise

them up on the last day; for my flesh is true food and my blood is true drink. Those who munch my flesh and drink my blood remain in me, and I in them. (John 6:51, 53-56)

While the Synoptics and Paul speak about Jesus' body (Greek *sōma*), the Fourth Gospel has Jesus speak of his flesh (Greek *sarx*), a much more physical image. Similarly, where the former speak of "eat" (Greek *esthiō*), the ordinary word for consuming food, John's Jesus speaks of *trōgō*, translated here as "munch" to highlight its affinity with the physical activity of chewing that is more graphic than simply "eating." John's Jesus speaks strongly because what is at issue for the Johannine community late in the first century was willingness (or unwillingness) to be known by one's neighbors as a regular participant in the *ekklēsia*'s life. It was not formal threats from imperial officials but the more insidious gossiping and reputation destruction from neighbors that made people hesitant to profess openly trust in Jesus and his God. Throughout John's Gospel, there is a tremendous tension between believing in Jesus secretly and being willing to "come out" publicly as a disciple. One might hide the fact of one's baptism from suspicious neighbors or customers, but one would be less able to remain secretive about one's frequent participation in a meal understandably construed by outsiders as cannibalistic. John's Jesus uses powerful language to insist that one must actually take part in the physical eating and drinking that make up the eucharistic assembly. More than any other New Testament writer, John equates the bread with Jesus' flesh. We should be careful about taking John's Gospel too literally on this point. After all, Jesus also says in this Gospel that he is a vine and a door! But, however one understands the relationship between bread and Jesus, it is absolutely certain that it means joining with others to celebrate the life-giving power of Jesus, remembered and found in the breaking of bread within the *ekklēsia*.

Thus, the Gospels and Paul's letters together show Eucharist as an occasion for the rejoining of the "body politic" with a "political body." The *ekklēsia* that gathers around and *becomes* Jesus' body proclaims its allegiance to a source of life different from that offered by empire. While the Gospel texts portray an exclusively Jewish gathering around Jesus' bread-body, Paul clearly understands this call to include people from any nation who seek to identify themselves with this alternative life source. We will see in the next chapter the implications of this form of worship for the new social and economic relationships that comprise the life of the *ekklēsiai*. For just as Passover was a memorial meant to instill a renewed sense of peoplehood in its participants, Eucharist likewise was a celebration intended to generate a freedom expressed in the practical aspects of daily life.

Footwashing

As noted, only John's Gospel moves the memory of Jesus' identification of himself with bread away from the Last Supper. In place of the question of Eucharist, it narrates Jesus' washing the disciples' feet and his command that they wash one another's feet (John 13). Given the powerful and already old association between the Last Supper and the Eucharist, John must have understood footwashing to be of equal importance. It is not mentioned anywhere else in the New Testament, however, nor is it frequently discussed by second- or third-century Christian writers as an essential practice of the *ekklēsia*. I think it worth including in this discussion, though, because its purpose responds to a need greatly felt in the church today.

Most Christians' initial sense of the reason for Jesus' washing of the disciples' feet and commanding them to do likewise was to teach them to be humble servants. However, when the footwashing is considered within the context of John's Gospel, it is clear that this is not its central meaning. Jesus, knowing that his earthly ministry is nearly over and that he will be killed the next day, needed to prepare his disciples to continue without him. John's Gospel narrates five chapters in which Jesus does this, frequently known as the Last Supper or Farewell Discourse (chaps. 13-17).

Throughout this long narrative, the disciples are portrayed as frightened and confused. Jesus offers them consolation in many ways: the gift of the Paraclete/Holy Spirit, the awareness that their suffering will be in solidarity with his own, the knowledge that the one Jesus calls Father is within and among them always. But the one thing he tells them to *do,* right at the outset of the speech, is to become a footwashing community. When examined closely, it becomes clear that his purpose is to teach them to *know one another* just as the Father and Jesus know one another. This is *biblical* knowledge, like that shared by Adam and Eve. In other words, they are to become intimate "friends" of Jesus and of one another (John 15:13-15). We will look more at this in chapter 3. But for the purpose of considering worship and liturgy, we should note that Jesus is not just giving a talk; he is establishing a ritual practice. He is turning their attention away from himself and toward one another, so that they can truly find the Risen One in their midst and thus continue his work of witness (John 20:18-20, 26).

Like other rituals that convey grace and strengthen the *ekklēsia,* footwashing was intended to be what would later be called a *sacrament.* Those who have participated in a footwashing in today's church know how powerful an experience it can be literally to hold another person in one's hands and lovingly caress their feet with warm water and a soft towel. Although we cannot be sure that the early *ekklēsia* beyond the Johannine community practiced footwashing regularly, it remains part of the New Testament tradition of what it meant to be church together.

Forgiveness of Sins and Debts

One of the central dramas in the Hebrew Scriptures is the constant abandonment by Israel of its exclusive loyalty to YHWH, and YHWH's equally constant willingness to forgive Israel and accept "her" back. In the big picture, the prophets speak often of God's and Israel's relationship as a marriage, with God as the cuckolded but forgiving spouse. But in the smaller picture of interpersonal life, how were people to repair their estranged or broken relationship with God and with one another?

The Torah provides a wide variety of procedures for overcoming one's status as a sinner. As one might expect, the legal aspect of Torah is most apparent here: specific acts are prohibited as "sins," and specific acts serve as reparation for those sins. One thing shines clearly through the entire body of Torah legislation: only God can grant forgiveness for one's sins, although the priests can mediate the process in accordance with Torah procedures. Thus, the official mechanism of forgiveness was entirely focused on Jerusalem and its Temple system.

What did this mean either for poor people in Galilee who could not come to Jerusalem or Israelites in the Diaspora? Often it meant living with a sense of not being right with God, that is, not practicing "righteousness" (Hebrew *tsedaqah*). It was in response to this apparent "injustice" that the Pharisees in Judea developed an oral tradition that allowed the process to take place closer to home. But they were in absolute agreement with the written Torah that God alone could grant forgiveness.

The later books of the Septuagint, though, written for Israelites far from Jerusalem, give a hint or two that there might also be a way in which one's personal relationships with others played a part in the process. For instance, we hear in Sirach:

> Anger and wrath, these also are abominations, and the sinful man will possess them. . . . Forgive [Greek *aphes*] your neighbor the wrong he has done, and then your sins will be pardoned [Greek *lythēsontai*] when you pray. (Sir. 27:30; 28:2)

The key Greek verbs Sirach uses are *hiēmi* as "forgive" and *lyō* as "pardon." The first is closely related to the common New Testament verb, *aphiēmi*, literally meaning "to let go" or "to send off." Sirach's second verb literally means "to loose," and is also frequent in the New Testament as a metaphor of forgiveness. Since both of these verbs are taken from the secular realm and applied to divine prerogatives in the Septuagint, we must assume that the New Testament usage is intended to recall the biblical context of forgiveness.

Into this context Jesus throws more than one bomb. By the second chapter of Mark's Gospel, Jesus has aroused the wrath of the scribes in Galilee for declaring a paralytic boy's sins forgiven. As they rightly see it according to the tradition, "Why does this fellow speak in this way? It is blasphemy! Who can forgive sins but God alone?" (Mark 2:7). Jesus not only claims that as the Human One, he shares in the divine power to forgive sins, but he tells his followers to do likewise in words that seem to echo the sentiments of Sirach: "Whenever you stand praying, forgive, if you have anything against anyone; so that your Father in heaven may also forgive you your trespasses" (Mark 11:25). The specific context for this teaching in Mark is immediately after the fig tree Jesus had cursed is found to be "withered to the roots." Between the cursing and the discovery, Jesus went through the Temple precincts shutting down operations and declaring that what was supposed to be "a house of prayer for all the nations" has been made by the Temple establishment into "a den of robbers" (Mark 11:15-17). Thus, in place of the corrupt Temple system, which devours the houses of widows and offers long prayers as a cover-up, Jesus invites the *ekklēsia* to seek rightness with God not in institutional functions but in forgiveness of one another. According to Mark's Jesus, no priests are required for this process.

Matthew and Luke elaborate on this tradition. In Matthew, Peter asks Jesus about the quantitative limits of forgiveness: "Lord, if another member of the *ekklēsia* sins against me, how often should I forgive? As many as seven times?" (Matt. 18:21). We should note that to forgive someone seven times evidences tremendous generosity of heart. How few people can manage that! But Jesus' response transforms quantity into quality: "Not seven times, but, I tell you, seventy-seven times," or in some translations, "seventy times seven times." In other words, it's not an accounting problem, but a matter of *unconditional love* (cf. Luke 17:3-4). The specific reference is likely to the primal cry for vengeance expressed by Lamech, descendant of Cain: "If Cain is avenged sevenfold, truly Lamech seventy-sevenfold" (Gen. 4:24). Thus, Jesus' call for unlimited forgiveness is made to reverse the "fallen" practice of unlimited vengeance.

This principle linking God's forgiveness of us to our willingness to forgive one another is, of course, at the heart of the Lord's Prayer tradition (Matt. 6:12-15; Luke 6:37; cf. John 20:23). It is one of the clearest principles in the New Testament, with echoes throughout the epistle tradition too (e.g., 2 Cor. 2:5-10; Eph. 4:32; Col. 3:12-13; 1 John 1:9). What stands in stark contrast to the Torah and later church practice is that there is no designation of official persons to mediate God's forgiveness. What began in the Torah as a *legal* procedure to rectify one's relationship with the unseen God has become an *interpersonal* procedure in relation to one's fellow *ekklēsia* member, or even one's enemies (Matt. 5:44; cf. Luke 23:34; Acts 7:60). To be the church means to practice forgiveness daily, disciple to disciple, so that the image of Christ can be seen in us as a body.

And in addition to offering a fresh start to one's personal relationships, disciples were also expected to provide one another forgiveness of *material* debts as a concrete expression of jubilee within the *ekklēsia,* to be discussed in chapter 3. Such forgiveness was not a matter of advancing a particular economic theory, but was a behavior flowing directly out of *prayer,* both that of the community as noted above, and of each disciple in his or her own daily spiritual practice.

Personal Prayer

The New Testament provides many images and sayings about the importance and power of prayer as a personal discipline in the life of each *ekklēsia* member. The only specific verbal prayer Jesus teaches is, of course, the one known as the Lord's Prayer. In Luke, a disciple asks Jesus to teach them to pray. This does not imply that the disciples otherwise knew nothing about prayer. As people raised in the biblical tradition, they would be very familiar with the Psalms and other prayers from Israel's treasury of faith. Their request of Jesus is for a specific "signature" prayer that would mark them as his followers, just as other popular religious teachers had a specific prayer that identified their followers. In Matthew, Jesus presents the prayer to them as part of the Sermon on the Mount, the compendium of wisdom teachings that are Matthew's distillation of Jesus' entire message. In Luke the prayer is part of the Sermon on the Plain. Both versions show how the basic thrust of prayer for Jesus' followers was to put complete trust in God rather than empire for everything they needed in daily life. Let's briefly compare the two versions:

Matthew 6:9-13	*Luke 11:2-4*
Our Father in heaven, hallowed be your name.	Father, hallowed be your name.
Your kingdom come.	Your kingdom come.
Your will be done, on earth as it is in heaven.	
Give us this day our daily bread.	Give us each day our daily bread.
And forgive us our debts [Greek *opheilēmata*],	And forgive us our sins [Greek *hamartias*],
as we also have forgiven our debtors.	for we ourselves forgive everyone indebted [Greek *opheilonti*] to us.
And do not bring us to the time of trial,	And do not bring us to the time of trial.
but rescue us from the evil one.	

There are several differences between the two versions. First, Matthew refers to "heaven" as the place where God is and where God's will is done. He also adds the petition for rescue from the evil one. Further, he begins with a first person plural address: "Our" Father. Thus, while the prayer can be said by individuals, it is always the prayer of the *ekklēsia* as well. Further, Matthew speaks of seeking and receiving forgiveness of *debts*, using a Greek

word understood both in the secular Greek world and in the Septuagint as referring to economic obligations (Deut. 24:10). Luke,
on the other hand, mixes his terms, seeking divine pardon of *sins*
in relation to one's own forgiveness of *debts*. In either case, one's
receipt of forgiveness is dependent on one's offering of jubilee
debt-release to others.

While both versions contain a set of petitions in the imperative
form—*demands* made on God—Matthew's Jesus prefaces his pre-
sentation by telling the disciples that they should not be like the
Gentiles who "heap up empty phrases," because God "knows what
you need before you ask" (Matt. 6:7-8). Thus, it is clear that the
petitions are not so much for the sake of persuading God to act in
a certain way as for the sake of lifting the disciples' minds and
hearts to God. In the face of imperial claims of "fatherhood"
(both the individual emperor and the state itself under the doctrine of *parens patriea*), Jesus has the disciples engage in daily
reminders that God alone deserves that title. In confrontation
with Roman provisions of "bread and circuses" to placate the
hungry multitude, the prayer seeks to inspire the recognition that
it is God who gives bread each day, just as God gave the manna in
the wilderness in the midst of the Israelites' nostalgic and grumbling yearnings for Egyptian provisions. In the midst of a patronage system that remembered each detail of economic and social
obligation, disciples are to forgive and seek forgiveness of all sins
and debts. Finally, Jesus urges them to pray to be saved from "the
time of trial," a not-so-veiled reference to the kind of imperial
persecution that Jesus faced (Luke 22:40, 46; cf. Acts 20:19).

Together, these petitions form the backbone of the *ekklēsia*'s
prayer life, a kind of "mission statement" that they are to recite
individually and collectively on a daily basis. As the Shema (Deut.
6:4-6) formed the central prayer for Israelites (which is affirmed
by Jesus [Mark 12:30; Matt. 22:37; Luke 10:27]), the Lord's Prayer
is the basis for unity among members of the *ekklēsia* throughout
the world.

But prayer is certainly not limited to this specific form. The
Greek verb for prayer (*proseuchomai*) is found eighty-five times in

the New Testament, while the noun (*proseuchē*) is used thirty-six times. Further, Jesus often uses the more ordinary words for "ask" or "request" in the context of petitioning God in prayer (e.g., John 14:13-16; 15:16; 16:24-26). One of Paul's closing words expresses the essence of the New Testament's sense of the role and context of prayer in the life of discipleship:

> Always seek to do good to one another and to all. Rejoice always, pray without ceasing, give thanks in all circumstances; for this is the will of God in Christ Jesus for you. (1 Thess. 5:15-18)

Four things are to be done "always": doing good, rejoicing, praying, and giving thanks. This is the "air" that the *ekklēsia* is to breathe amidst the thick smog of imperial propaganda. Such spiritual practice enables many things that would otherwise be "impossible" for humans (e.g., Mark 9:23; 10:27). For example:

- Casting out demons and unclean spirits (Mark 9:29)

- Healing the sick (Jas. 5:13-16)

- Keeping the faith while church members are in jail (Acts 12:5; 16:25)

- Discerning the difference between God's will and one's own (Mark 14:35-36; Acts 1:24-26)

- Receiving unexpected joy and gladness (Luke 1:13-14)

- Receiving visions from "the other side of the veil" (Acts 10:2-6, 9-16; Rev. 1:10ff.)

This kind of constant praying is clearly not a function of certain office holders but a responsibility and privilege of every disciple in the *ekklēsia*. Without it, the *ekklēsia* can quickly become simply a social club, of which there were many in the Mediterranean cities. It is daily prayer to the one Jesus called "Abba"/ Daddy that keeps the *ekklēsia* true to its call.

Communal Discernment of Spirits

One aspect of the early *ekklēsia*'s worldview that differs substantially from that of our time is the presumption that reality is suffused with a diversity of spiritual beings. Angels and demons have been largely banished from our rationalistic conception of the universe, although recently angels have been making a comeback. Our modern world has "explained" as mental or other illness various manifestations that the New Testament attributes to "unclean spirits," while other phenomena are viewed as leftovers of a "primitive" mythic perspective for which there is no room in the modern mind.

Is it the case, however, that Jesus possessed a "primitive" mindset? Were the New Testament writers captive to an outdated way of understanding the world? Recently, psychologist-theologians such as Walter Wink have encouraged us to rethink our banishment of "spirits." Wink's *Powers* trilogy has dramatically reopened the door for a renewed understanding of the reality of such invisible entities. In any event, there is no doubt that the early *ekklēsia* took the existence of such spirits totally for granted.

One implication of this we will examine in chapter 5 as we consider healing and exorcism as part of the *ekklēsia*'s mission. But whether to recognize unclean or evil spirits and cast them out, or simply to know for sure when one is being guided by the Holy Spirit, the *ekklēsia* needed to learn how to discern among the various spirits present in the world. Paul states clearly that "discernment of spirits" is one of the key gifts of the Holy Spirit given for the "common good" of the *ekklēsia* (1 Cor. 12:7, 10). The Greek word translated "discernment," *diakrisis*, means literally "judgment across," that is, to decide or distinguish among options. While this specific word is uncommonly used in the New Testament, it points toward the wider practice of praying for clarity in a situation in which many spirits call out to be obeyed, including the spirit of empire, which pervaded and continues to pervade all of daily life.

For example, in Acts we see an express instance of this as the *ekklēsia* prays to replace Judas: "Lord, you know everyone's heart. Show us which one of these two you have chosen to take the place in this ministry and apostleship from which Judas turned aside" (Acts 1:24). When the *ekklēsia* must decide whether Gentiles must adopt Jewish cultural practices and how much they will be required to withdraw from imperial ones, it comes together in prayerful discernment, reaching a result grounded in that prayer (Acts 15:1-22). It is precisely this which distinguishes the assembly of the Way from the secular *ekklēsia* of the Greeks: the attempt not to persuade others through powerful rhetoric or "worldly wisdom" but to listen for the call of the Holy Spirit (cf. 1 Cor. 2).

The author of First John provides another classic example of the need for discernment of spirits.

> Beloved, do not trust every spirit, but test the spirits to see whether they are from God; for many false prophets have gone out into the world. By this you know the Spirit of God: every spirit that confesses that Jesus Christ has come in the flesh is from God. (1 John 4:1-2)

The pastoral situation addressed by this letter was a particularly difficult one: a strong disagreement in the *ekklēsia* over Jesus' human essence had led to a split in the community in which some members quit. The temptation to maintain unity at any cost—especially when the *ekklēsia* was such a drop in the imperial bucket anyway—must have been great. But the writer of the epistle insists that the *ekklēsia* discern between the Spirit of God and what he calls "antichrist" (the only place in the New Testament where this word is used). It is powerful language indeed, and yet it is evoked because the writer believes the stakes could not be higher. The practical nature of *love* is on the line. If Jesus was not really "in the flesh," then there is no model of love which truly lays down its physical life for friends (1 John 3:16; 4:6-21). The writer insists that, despite their claim to be possessed by the same spirit as the other *ekklēsia* members, those who have left in denial of

Jesus' fleshly reality were in fact possessed by a spirit in opposition to Christ. The visible test that confirms the result of this discernment of spirits is thus whether or not one truly loves one's brothers and sisters in the *ekklēsia* by treating them with nonviolence (1 John 3:11-18; 4:20).

In a similar vein, the book of Revelation begins with messages from the risen Jesus to the "angels" of the seven *ekklēsia* in Roman Asia (Rev. 2-3). The messages express blame and praise for each angel's fidelity or lack thereof to God's Way in the face of numerous temptations to conform to the imperial ethos. But note that the messages are not directed to individual persons or even to the *ekklēsia* directly, but to the "angel" of each *ekklēsia*. Just as the Greeks and Romans believed that each city or other institution had a guardian *daemon* (the generic Greek word for a spiritual being, not expressing a negative value judgment as does the English "demon"), so Jesus tells John to speak Jesus' words to the guardian spirit of each city's *ekklēsia*. In this kind of discernment, it is not a matter of "good" angels versus "evil" ones, but of each angel's mixed ability to remain true to its call. Jesus says, for example, to the angel of the *ekklēsia* at Ephesus that if the angel does not practice *metanoia*, Jesus will "take away your lampstand" (Rev. 2:5; cf. 1:20). In other words, "Shape up, angel, or I'll get someone else for this job!" The conception of a guardian spirit is not that of a puppeteer pulling strings, but of the collective essence of the individual members gathered as a single *ekklēsia*, just as the soul or personality of an individual person expresses the unity of intention and action of arms, legs, heart, and so forth. Each *ekklēsia* must constantly discern which spirit it is obeying as it expresses itself in daily action in the world.

Bible Study

A final aspect of the *ekklēsia*'s worshipful activity is its prayerful study and reflection on its sacred stories. While Bible study has taken a back seat in recent years to other practices of spiritual formation, it is clear that without it, the *ekklēsia* can quickly lose its way. For instance, in the encounter on the road to Emmaus, Jesus, after listening to the two disciples' story of disappointment and loss, declares them "foolish" because they have not done their Bible study (Luke 24:25-27). Similarly, characters in Acts repeatedly explain Jesus to their Jewish audiences in terms of fulfillment of the law and prophets (e.g., 3:18, 21, 24; 7:42, 52; 10:43, etc.). Paul's whole message is grounded in his belief that the resurrection of Jesus is the fulfillment of all that was promised by God in the Hebrew Scriptures (e.g., Acts 26:22; Rom. 1:1-4). He goes so far as to say that the central reason for the Jerusalem leaders and their supporters' handing over of Jesus to the Romans was their failure to do good Bible study (Acts 13:27)!

Beyond these express admonitions to study the scriptures, the New Testament is truly incomprehensible apart from the Hebrew Scriptures, of which it forms but a branch. To call Jesus "Christ"/Messiah could make no sense at all to a Greco-Roman Gentile in the absence of extensive instruction in the Hebrew Scriptures. This is one reason that texts such as Matthew's and John's Gospels so frequently refer explicitly to the fulfillment of scripture. Without these narrative "hints," the authors assume that their audiences would miss the point. In contrast, Revelation never expressly quotes Hebrew Scripture, and yet much modern incomprehension of its images stems from lack of familiarity with the scriptural subtexts out of which its apocalyptic mosaic is composed. Hardly a verse in Revelation does not pull forward at least one image or phrase from Hebrew Scriptures. Without a constant "this was to fulfill" or "as the prophet X said," someone who has not been immersed in the Bible can easily find Revelation hopelessly confusing and obscure. But for those who have practiced the Deuteronomic injunction to make scripture part of one's daily life (Deut. 6:6-9), reading Revelation leads to an incessant refrain of "we've heard all this before!"

The biblical study and reflection method engaged in by these New Testament writers is what is known in Jewish circles of interpretation as *midrash* (pl. *midrashim*). The term comes from the

Hebrew *derash* meaning "to search," and thus, to interpret sacred texts in light of later experience and vice versa. Peter, Stephen, and Paul each are shown engaged in *midrash* in their speeches in Acts (e.g., Acts 2:16-21 [interpreting the Pentecost event from a text of the prophet Joel]; 7:20-44 [interpreting the Sanhedrin's resistance in light of resistance of Moses]; 13:32-37 [interpreting Jesus' resurrection in light of Psalm 2]). We saw above how Jesus reinterpreted the manna tradition in Exodus 16 in light of his provision of his own flesh as food (John 6:31-58).

Furthermore, many Gospel narratives are implicit *midrashim* on older scripture texts. For example, Jesus' provision of wine at a wedding reinterprets the prophetic proclamation of the abundance of "sweet wine" in the messianic era (John 2:1-11, interpreting, e.g., Joel 3:18; Amos 9:13), and his wellside encounter with a Samaritan woman is built on the patriarchal well-courtship traditions (John 4:4-42, interpreting Gen. 24:11-51; 29:1-20). The practice of *midrash* pointed not only to the value of the old stories for interpreting life but to the living nature of God's Word, which could not be contained in the written texts but called for constant revitalization through studied exegesis *and* prophetic action.

One of the boldest claims by the *ekklēsia* was that its own stories about Jesus and the Spirit shared in the sacred status of "Word of God" along with the Torah, prophets, and writings of Hebrew Scripture. The Gospel writers did not know a collection called the "New Testament," and many texts described as "Gospels" did not make the canonical cut when the final determination was made centuries later as to which writings would be included and which would not. One expects that Paul might be shocked and dismayed to discover that his pastoral letters, which were addressed to specific needs of particular communities, would later be received as a source of universal wisdom for *ekklēsia* members. But long before these formal decisions were made, the *ekklēsia* knew that both its self-understanding and its ongoing discernment of mission could take place only in an environment constantly suffused with the Word of God. As the

Israelites called on the experiences and stories of their ancestors in order to discern how to live in later circumstances, so too did the *ekklēsia* come to rely on both the Israelites' traditions and their own for guidance. This implied, as it did for ancient Israel, a constant tension between the written and oral word, the sacredness of the tradition, and the constant newness of God that broke through old formulations (cf. Deut. 4:2 and 12:32 with Deut. 18:15-18). Regardless of which written texts were to be selected for inclusion in the eventual biblical canon, the *ekklēsiai* knew that there would be ongoing need for interpretation of the old and openness to the new Word as spoken and as lived.

With all these tools and rituals available, the *ekklēsia* could go about the process of discerning how it was to be structured, who and how important functions were to be performed, and how it was to preach and practice the Good News in the midst of a broken world overflowing with sorrow and suffering.

Reflection Questions

1. What feelings and thoughts do you bring to the idea of "going to church"? Why do you or don't you attend organized religious services? What expectations do you have about the relationship between church worship and the "world out there"? How might those expectations be similar to or different from those of the first *ekklēsiai*?

2. What rituals bond you to those with whom you feel most connected? Consider, for example,

   (a) shared meals or beverages (e.g., going out for drinks or coffee, having tea, as well as more complete meals)

   (b) attendance at or participation in sporting events

   (c) watching television, listening to music, or sharing other forms of popular culture

(d) shopping

(e) civic participation (e.g., secular holidays such as Thanksgiving or Fourth of July; attending political activities and
events)

(f) rituals of your own creation (e.g., making music, storytelling, playing games)

(g) "religious" activities beyond formal worship (e.g., Bible
study, prayer group)

How do these rituals function similarly to or differently from
those of the early *ekklēsia?* How do your favorite rituals affirm or
challenge your allegiance to some form of shared identity (e.g.,
membership in nation or city, fans of a team or a branded product, part of a family or circle of friends)?

3. What role does prayer, both individual and communal, play
in your life? Do you think it is "effective"? Why or why not? What
does the New Testament admonition to pray "always" mean to
you? What difference does it make, if any, to pray with others
rather than in solitude?

3

Brothers and Sisters in Christ

The Ekklēsia *as God's Household*

In identifying the discipleship community as an *ekklēsia*, the first followers of Jesus chose from a dizzying array of models, both biblical and Greco-Roman, for social organizations. As we saw in chapter 1, *ekklēsia* was rooted in images and ideas from both Hebrew Scriptures and Greek society. Yet one of the most radical ways in which disciples distinguished themselves from other urban dwellers was in calling each other "brothers" and "sisters." We will now explore the sources and implications of this set of relationships.

Perhaps a surprising starting point is to recognize that there is no word for what we would call "family" in the Hebrew Scriptures, the Septuagint, or the New Testament. The current movement to establish Christian "family values" as grounded in the Bible finds virtually no support. Consider, for example, these images of "family" from the New Testament:

A crowd was sitting around him; and they said to him, "Your mother and your brothers and sisters are outside, asking for you." And he replied, "Who are my mother and my brothers?" And looking at those who sat around him, he said, "Here are my mother and my brothers! Whoever does the will of God is my brother and sister and mother." (Mark 3:32-35)

When his parents saw him they were astonished; and his mother said to him, "Child, why have you treated us like this? Look, your father and I have been searching for you in great anxiety." He said to them, "Why were you searching for me? Did you not know that I must be in my Father's house?" But they did not understand what he said to them. (Luke 2:48-50)

To another he said, "Follow me." But he said, "Lord, first let me go and bury my father." But Jesus said to him, "Let the dead bury their own dead; but as for you, go and proclaim the kingdom of God." Another said, "I will follow you, Lord; but let me first say farewell to those at my home." Jesus said to him, "No one who puts a hand to the plow and looks back is fit for the kingdom of God." (Luke 9:59-62)

So his brothers said to him, "Leave here and go to Judea so that your disciples also may see the works you are doing; for no one who wants to be widely known acts in secret. If you do these things, show yourself to the world." (For not even his brothers trusted in him.) Jesus said to them, "My time has not yet come, but your time is always here. The world cannot hate you, but it hates me because I testify against it that its works are evil." (John 7:3-7)

I have come to set a person against his or her father, and a daughter against her mother, and a daughter-in-law against her mother-in-law; and one's foes will be members of one's own household. Whoever loves father or mother more than me is not worthy of me; and whoever loves son or daughter more than me is not worthy of me. (Matt. 10:35-37)

From these passages we can see that all the Gospels are clear that what we think of as family is to be subordinated to one's relationships with God and the members of the *ekklēsia*. How would this model play among Jews or Gentiles in the Greco-Roman cities?

"Family Values" in the Hebrew Scriptures

First let's look briefly at the Hebrew Scriptures' sense of family. As noted earlier, the smallest social unit in Israel was the *bet ʾab*, or "father's house." This term is more broad than our sense of nuclear or even extended family in that it included servants and sojourners residing with a particular kinship group. The Hebrew Scriptures do not idealize the harmony and sanctity of these social building blocks. In fact, they almost systematically undermine one's perception of the household as a place of peace, love, and justice. The Genesis narratives are the most condensed collection of "family" stories, and yet not one of those households would we uphold as a model to emulate. Abraham and Sarah fight over their children Ishmael and Isaac, just as Isaac and Rebekah play favorites between Esau and Jacob. Abraham is willing to kill his beloved son to appease God. Rebekah and Jacob (or perhaps Rebekah and Isaac) team up to rip away the firstborn son Esau's blessing and birthright. Esau plots to kill his only brother in revenge. Later, Jacob squabbles with and deceives his uncle Laban, who had previously tricked him into twenty years of hard labor. Finally, Jacob's sons in turn plot murder against their younger brother Joseph, who cooks up a complex plan to twist the family's emotions into knots. And let's not forget Cain and Abel!

The other major "family story" in Hebrew Scriptures is that of David and his children. Here we find such "family values" as incest, rape, fratricide and attempted parricide, not to mention David's adulterous ways. Yet David, far from condemned, remains God's beloved favorite, whose descendant is to be the longed-for Messiah. These examples are not isolated stories, but are among the most treasured narratives in the Hebrew Scriptures. There simply is no model in the Bible for what we might think of as an "ideal family."

Having said that, it does remain the case that one's relationships with one's blood kin were the ones for which one was expected to risk death. In Genesis, we see Abraham engaging in a military campaign to rescue his nephew Lot from enemy captivity (Gen. 14) and Jacob's sons pursuing a scorched-earth policy of murder and pillage to rescue their sister Dinah from the neighboring Shechemites (Gen. 34). Except in the first generations, before there were great numbers of Israelites, marriage or other interaction outside the "people of Israel" was a serious violation of Torah (e.g., Deut. 7:1-6). Although Deuteronomy speaks as if its audience members were all literal descendants of the "founding father" Jacob/Israel, it was certainly true that by the time the text was written, "Israel" included many former members of other peoples from throughout Canaan and perhaps other lands such as Egypt and Mesopotamia.

During the period of Israel's existence prior to the monarchy, it was the family household and the association of households known as the *mishpachah*, or "clan," in which people found their primary identity, as discussed in chapter 1. The linking of such households through stories of common ancestors and their protective deity—such as Abraham and Sarah and their God, El/YHWH—extended the sense of community beyond blood ties to include all those bonded in a common purpose. The biblical "family stories" reflect the actual difficulties of life in the precarious situation of reliance on YHWH alone in a subsistence economy. To survive required feeling deeply connected to people upon whom one's very life depended. This sense of "fictive kin"—people unrelated by blood but bonded by shared stories of origin and lived experiences—was the primary vehicle for maintaining a sense of "peoplehood" among the various clans and tribes that lived in Canaan throughout the period reported in the book of Judges.

With the monarchy, the Jerusalem elite put tremendous pressure on these basic life units to see the nation-state as the primary, unifying social reality. As we have seen, the unity and solidarity of household and clan were frequently torn apart by the needs of Israel's imperial regime for workers and wealth. Efforts to centralize worship in Jerusalem eroded people's sense of the local presence and working of divine power. Yet the enduring strength of the local households and clans survived even the most sweeping of "reforms," namely, King Josiah's systematic campaign to destroy local shrines and holy places and to transform Passover into a Jerusalem pilgrimage feast rather than the household-based celebration it had been (2 Kgs. 23:1-25).

For those who remained in the land after the destruction first of the northern kingdom of Israel and later of the southern kingdom of Judah, the pressure to conform to Jerusalem's wishes was temporarily relieved. However, the program of centralization was reinitiated by those who returned from Babylonian exile to reestablish a community devoted to YHWH in Jerusalem. The notion of fictive kin was called upon by the returnees in the priest Ezra's official command to "separate yourselves from the peoples of the land and from the foreign wives." (Ezra 10:11). To maintain a sense of "foreign" after two generations in Babylon meant holding on to this sense of kin, defined as those who have committed to the covenant with and worship of YHWH alone, regardless of actual historical bloodlines. To support this reestablishment, the returnees developed a detailed set of genealogies linking the new residents of Jerusalem with the "ancestral houses" (Hebrew *bet ʾaboth*, literally, "fathers' house," used in lists at, e.g., Ezra 10:15-44; 1 Chr. 6). In sum, whether the actual village-based households and clans of premonarchic or rural Israel, or the genealogical identity used by the postexilic builders of Jerusalem's new community, the Hebrew Scriptures show a consistent practice of envisioning those with whom one shared the covenant with YHWH as members of one's "household."

It is this image and tradition of "household" that is tapped into by the New Testament writers in referring to fellow disciples as "brothers" and "sisters." As we saw in the passage from Mark's Gospel above, Jesus is quoted as saying that "brother and sister" are to be defined not by blood but by "doing the will of God." While disciples will likely experience great tension within their blood families because of their commitment to the gospel, they will gain a new family in membership in the *ekklēsia* (cf. John 9:18-23, 35-38). This is one of the underlying connotations of the New Testament references to the *ekklēsia* as a new "Israel" or as "the people of God" (e.g., Rom. 9-11; Gal. 6:15-16; Rev. 7).

The *ekklēsia* thus saw itself in continuity with the historical Israelite sense of being called out of empire to be God's own people. Members were expected to see each other as bonded by a glue stronger than blood: the very will of the Creator. Luke, in fact, uses the Greek verb *kollaō*, meaning literally "to glue oneself," when he speaks in Acts of people joining the *ekklēsia* (Acts 5:13; 8:29; 9:26; 10:28; 17:34). A Jew considering joining the *ekklēsia* might therefore understand himself or herself called to a commitment parallel to the ancient one establishing a people of God centuries earlier.

The biggest difference between the historical people of Israel gathered as *ekklēsia* and that of Jesus' followers was the criteria for inclusion. Scholars continue to argue about whether Jesus in his earthly ministry ever intended his message for those outside of the ethnic group of Israel (e.g., Matt. 10:5-6; 15:21-28). But it is undoubtedly the case that one of the major theological breakthroughs in the early *ekklēsia* was that "God's people" was not to be based on any kind of inherited social or cultural distinction. In Paul's ringing "emancipation proclamation," "there is no longer Jew or Greek, there is no longer slave or free, there is no longer male and female; for all of you are one in Christ Jesus" (Gal. 3:28; cf. Col. 3:11). The first part of this proclamation, of course, was scandalous, even blasphemous, to the ears of a traditional Israelite, as the second and third parts would be to someone steeped in the Roman patronage system, as we will see below. Nonetheless, the New Testament writers are crystal clear in their understanding that the Jesus event and the coming of the Holy Spirit meant that old boundaries of ethnicity, class, and gender had been dissolved (e.g., John 4 [ethnicity]; Luke 16:19-31 [class];

Phil. 4:1-3 [gender]; generally, Acts 10:34-35). Across every kind of barrier established by human beings, God's people would now understand themselves to comprise a single, worldwide household (Greek *oikoumenē*, e.g., Matt. 24:14) responsible for caring for and loving each other as Jesus had loved them (e.g., John 13:34-35).

Within this new household, there was to be *no hierarchy*, a word taken from the Greek meaning "sacred leadership." Matthew's Jesus admonishes the *ekklēsia* to "call no one your father on earth, for you have one Father, the one in heaven" (Matt. 23:9). Similarly, the other Gospels repeatedly narrate Jesus reversing the usual social structure of power and authority and teaching his disciples to do the same (e.g., Mark 10:35-45). John's Gospel presents the image of the *ekklēsia* as branches, all gaining sustenance from the Vine, Jesus, with whom each one is individually and collectively bound.

Paul again and again insists on his social lowliness, despite his apparently educated background and, according to Luke, Roman citizenship. He insists that to claim authority over others on the basis of anything other than the power of the Spirit is to live according to the world's wisdom, not the wisdom of God (1 Cor. 2). He adapts a popular metaphor from Stoic philosophy—of the society as a body—in order to reinforce this point. In Stoic usage, the image of society-as-body was meant to *reinforce* social differentiation. "Of course," they might say, "the head is more important than the foot. Each person fits into his or her own place in the social structure, and some are just more 'fittingly' placed higher or lower." In Paul's version, though, it is the *unity* of the body that is central. Calling once again on his manifesto of one Spirit for both Jews and Greeks, slaves or free (1 Cor. 12:13), he "quotes" the "lowest" parts of the body according to the Stoic ideal only to refute it: "If the foot would say, 'Because I am not a hand, I do not belong to the body,' that would not make it any less a part of the body" (1 Cor. 12:15). In fact, he says, the truth in Christ is exactly the opposite of the Stoic concept:

The eye cannot say to the hand, "I have no need of you," nor again the head to the feet, "I have no need of you." On the contrary, the members of the body that seem to be weaker are indispensable, and those members of the body that we think less honorable we clothe with greater honor, and our less respectable members are treated with greater respect; whereas our more respectable members do not need this. But God has so arranged the body, giving the greater honor to the inferior member, that there may be no dissension within the body, but the members may have the same care for one another. (1 Cor. 12:21-25)

The *ekklēsia*, in other words, was in continuity with the inherited biblical understanding that only God was worthy of power and honor and that all members of the community were of equal value in God's sight. But it was breaking radically new ground to include within this relationship persons from "every tribe and language and people and nation" (Rev. 5:9, also 7:9; 14:6). Those considered "least" according to any worldly standard would now be full-fledged members of a new sister and brotherhood of God.

Family in the Greco-Roman Context

How, though, would this kind of social commitment have been received among one's Gentile neighbors and associates? The Greco-Roman urban environment was awash in a diversity of associational forms. There were many factors pushing people to find bonds with one another. The city population was usually a mixture of peoples from various locales, separated from their places of origin by war, slave-taking, famine, or economic takeover of ancestral farmland by the imperial elite. While in the eastern empire Greek was the common language in the first century, not all spoke it with equal fluency. People carried with them a variety of so-called pagan (meaning "country folk") religions and other cultural practices that had previously served as social glue but now tended to isolate people from each other. We see, of course, a similar pattern in the United States today, where cultural diversity can both unite and divide within the wider social milieu. In addition to this sense of isolation and loneliness, the cities were also dangerous and dirty places. Economic insecurity forced many into petty and sometimes violent crime. Construction was not "up to code," and one faced enormous risk of accidental injury or even death just walking down the street or climbing the stairs to one's third-story apartment. Despite Roman improvements, sanitation was difficult at best and disease rampant. Finally, none of what the modern industrial world expects in terms of government and corporate institutional forms of security (police, fire, health care, retirement benefits, and so forth) were available. Whatever provisions for safety and future security one might want had to be carved out by hand, so to speak, from available resources.

The primary means that Greco-Roman society developed to handle this endemic insecurity was what scholars call the "patronage system." While this chapter divides the *ekklēsia*'s social and economic relationships from each other for schematic purposes, the patronage system provided a structure fully inclusive of both sectors of life. In a nutshell, it generated a pyramidal set of social and economic relationships. At the top, of course, were the wealthy elite: members of the Roman equestrian and senatorial classes. Persons below this narrow group linked with their "superiors" by exchanging *honor and loyalty* for access to *material resources*. This principle of exchange continued all the way through the society from the emperor to the lowest plebeian. Consider, for example, the desire of folks in Ephesus to build a temple to their revered goddess, Artemis. Where would the local elite find the wealth with which to acquire the enormous quantities of marble and other materials, along with the labor to transport the materials and construct the edifice? The answer was, "from above." In exchange for including statues of the emperor and his family within the Artemision (the Artemis temple)—and eventually, offering worship to the living emperor himself—the people of Ephesus got themselves a huge temple. The building was not simply a place of worship; it was, in the words of one ancient writer, "the common bank of Asia." In a world that did not separate religion from commerce, shrines and temples always served multiple functions as economic, social, and religious gathering places. Indeed, the entire patronage system was seen as supported by a plethora of divine beings, each "blessing" specific gatherings, places, and relationships. The patronage system was understood as simply a mirror of the relationships among the gods and goddesses themselves, with Zeus/Jupiter parallel to the emperor and with other parallels down the line.

How did ordinary people function in this system? For folks on the city streets scratching out a living, one might attach oneself to a local patron, much as churches and institutions of the arts do today. But rather than offering praise and thanksgiving in glossy magazines and on building plaques, people would literally meet the patron daily at the door and offer loud words of honor, often following the patron around to his or her next appointment. Those willing to participate in this system might gain a modicum of security and protection in the event of injury or economic disaster. Others, however, chose different ways to assuage danger and loneliness.

A general term for a variety of ways people came together for mutual support was the Latin *vici*, "associations," also known as *collegia*. These could be created under the bond of common labor or trade or other similar interests. They offered members—under the patronage of a deity or a person—mutual aid for basic needs such as burial and simple forms of worker compensation in the event of serious injury. They also provided occasion for special feasts and celebrations. Imperial authorities were generally suspicious of such associations, as they were of any "unnecessary" gathering that might be fomenting revolt. But given the large and dense urban populations, the *collegia* were more or less tolerated unless they gave specific reason for suspicion. They might consist of between thirty or forty and a few hundred members in a particular city.

We see an example of such an organization in Acts, where the Ephesian silversmiths come together under the patronage of the goddess Artemis to stir up opposition against Paul and his companions, whom they rightfully see as a threat to their business of making silver models of the Artemision for worshipers and tourists (Acts 19:24-41). Luke shows how easily the silversmiths could fill the local theater (which seated around 24,000 persons) with confused citizens who hardly know why they have been gathered. Note that in narrating the calming of the crowd, Luke has the local city official appeal to the processes of civic court and *ekklēsia* as a basis for avoiding the charge of rioting and achieving justice (19:38-40).

The near universal participation in patronage and local aid societies such as the *collegia* created a challenge to disciples of Jesus. Much of Paul's first letter to the Corinthians addresses issues arising from the Corinthian *ekklēsia* members trying to play both sides of the fence. Paul is utterly unwilling to support their ongoing efforts to achieve status and security by participation in the dominant culture if it means in any way compromising the integrity of the *ekklēsia* or the faith of its "weak" members. For example, he is shocked to find out that members have taken a business dispute to the Roman court system (1 Cor. 6). After rather sarcastically chastising them for their pursuit of Roman justice, he tells them, "In fact, to have lawsuits at all with one another is already a defeat for you. Why not rather be wronged? Why not rather be defrauded?" (1 Cor. 6:7) Paul knows all too well how rigged the Roman courts were on behalf of the rich and those who offered patronage to others. Even to participate in such a system was to betray the gospel.

Later in the letter, he similarly confronts the Corinthians' desire to attend banquets at the temples where worship and honor of local and Roman deities is *de rigueur* (1 Cor. 8-10). They argue, in effect, "Hey, we know the 'idols' aren't real, so it's no big deal to offer a little incense or a few prayers, as long as our fingers are crossed" (1 Cor. 8:4-5). But Paul appeals to the "perception of impropriety," that is, to the effect such behavior might have on those who know that these people claim to be *ekklēsia* members or those who aren't so clear on the falsity of the Greco-Roman religious practices. There is enough to drink from the cup of Christ, he tells them, to provide the nourishment you need (1 Cor. 10:16-21). If the *ekklēsia* is to be one body eating from one loaf, then it does not advance the program to seek status at the idol temples. In these and other passages, we see the strain and challenge of trying to be the people "called out" while surrounded by other cultural practices. But if one has joined the *ekklēsia* of Jesus, then one ought need no other patron—divine or human—or any other source of security.

One can already see in some of the later New Testament writings the pressure to conform the social relationships within the *ekklēsiai* to the structures of the surrounding cultures. While the biblical texts did not have a high regard for "family" as we idealize it today, the Roman household did. The basic social unit among Roman citizens and those aspiring to fit within Roman society was the *familia*, the patriarchal family. Within this model, there *was* a strong sense of hierarchy, with fathers over children, masters over slaves, and husbands over wives. To promote or, worse, to practice social arrangements according to Paul's proclamation in Galatians 3:28 was to draw attention to oneself and one's community as socially subversive. For some Christians of the generation after Paul, the desire to establish the church for the long term seemed to be in conflict with living the gospel in all its radicality. This struggle is not far from the one we experience in our day in which pastors attempt to balance keeping a congregation socially and financially viable without compromising the gospel "too much." In the late first century, we see one "solution" to this problem in what scholars call the "household code" in the letters to the Ephesians (5:21-6:9) and to the Colossians (3:18-4:1). It is found even more strongly in the latest New Testament documents, First Peter (3:1-7) and Titus (3:1-10). These texts urge the *ekklēsiai* in nearly identical language to live in this regard according to the message not of Jesus or Paul but of Roman society. Of course, such texts were not an "inevitable" or "evolutionary" development in the history of the church. Other writers, such as the authors of Revelation or John's Gospel, continued to maintain the position that the *ekklēsia*'s social structure should be derived solely from the gospel and not from Roman society. What the New Testament reveals is that then, as now, there was controversy and struggle over the relationship between the ordering of church in relation to the surrounding society.

Feminist writers have often criticized the texts that appear to support the Roman *familia* structure as expressing a patriarchal and oppressive stance toward women. This is a deserved charge, but to limit the focus to gender is to miss the larger point of these texts. The goal of these writers—claiming the mantle of Paul or Peter—is not the repression of women per se but the conformance of Christian conduct to the norms of empire. We see this clearly in the letter of Titus. After calling women and slaves to submission to husbands and masters, the writer continues by urging all "to be subject to rulers and authorities" (Titus 3:1). How far this is from the stories Luke tells in Acts, where, for example, Peter and Paul stand more than once in the dock for obeying God rather than human authorities (e.g., Acts 5:27-33)! Indeed, Jesus clearly expected the disciples to stand charged with violations of civil and religious law as the price for fidelity to the gospel (e.g., Mark 13:9-10; John 16:1-4). As we have seen, Jesus repeatedly announced his command *not* to be obedient to the demands of parents when they stood between oneself and obedience to God. But the temptation of these later writers to urge conformity with the imperial social standards is understandable. Both Jesus' and Paul's experiences witness to the physical and emotional suffering that true discipleship can require. And yet, by the beginning of the second century, Christian writers were once again celebrating a discipleship that led to martyrdom (e.g., Ignatius, *Ephesians*, chap. 1). This tension between the *ekklēsia*'s call to live socially subversive, egalitarian relationships as God's own children and the urge to "fit in" with the world has been with us ever since.

Israel's Heritage of Sabbatical and Jubilee Economics

The central topics of conversation and debate in many churches today are often far removed from those of the first *ekklēsiai*. Whereas abortion and sexuality are frequently the subject of church documents and proclamations in our world, the New Testament has relatively little to say about sexuality and never mentions abortion. On the other hand, we rarely hear discussed today what was one of, if not *the* primary, issue for the early *ekklēsia:* economics.

While we have seen that both the word and the concept of "family" as we know it was foreign to the entire biblical tradition, our word "economics" comes directly out of the ancient world. The Greek words *oikia nomos* mean "house law" and refer broadly to the rules and principles for dealing with the material *stuff* of daily life. We will see that the New Testament's apparently radical views on economics offer almost nothing new in *content* from the earlier biblical tradition. What is totally new, though, is the *context*: How were the people of God to live the economic lifeways enshrined in the Torah within the urban world of a foreign empire?

What were the economic principles that were intended to govern Israel's life? Before we look at the content, we must examine briefly the context of economic lawgiving in the Torah. After rules of priestly sacrifice, economic commandments are probably the most frequent topic of Torah legislation as well as narrative storytelling. Indeed, as Meir Sternberg has pointed out, we cannot fairly read the legal provisions of Torah as we might read a law code from our culture, that is, separated from the stories that generated the code itself and the stories of its being lived out. Hebrew Scripture contains not a "law code" but what Sternberg calls "nominarrative": *stories* about the giving and receiving of law amidst the experience of the wilderness wandering. The story-telling context of all Torah was the movement out of empire and into a liminal place where God alone had power and authority. The Israelites' challenge was to take this body of teachings given in the pure, harsh light of the desert and practice them in the more foggy environment of settled life in Canaan.

Many sociologists and historians searching for the roots of Israel's existence beyond the bounds of the biblical story have concluded that the primary motivation that generated "Israel" was the belief that YHWH, the Creator God, called forth a people to live in an egalitarian, economic community apart from the domination system of empire. Whether they came out of Egypt or the Canaanite city-states or both, the people who settled in the highlands of Canaan over three thousand years ago lived in a locale just about as far removed from empire as possible. Indeed, without the technological breakthroughs of lime-lined water cisterns and agricultural terracing, the rocky and desolate hill country of Canaan would have been uninhabitable. There is little archaeological evidence that any long-term settlements had been established in that land prior to those of the Israelites. It was apparently their belief that only in this difficult but relatively secure outpost could YHWH's ways be lived in peace. From this perspective, we can see how much of the Genesis and Exodus narrative leading up to the giving of the law on Mt. Sinai contrasts the relatively easy but "evil" life of those in the "well-watered" plains below with the closer-to-God but harsher life in the hills and mountains. For example, Abraham settles in the hills, but Lot in the plain of Sodom and Gomorrah, only to be rescued by God because of Abraham (Gen. 13, 18-19). Eden itself is a mountain-top setting *from* which the world's rivers flow, in contrast to paradise in Mesopotamian storytelling, which takes place in the valley *into* which the rivers flow. Egypt, like Sodom and Gomorrah, is well-watered, but its easy harvests lead to storage of surplus, slavery, and empire, while the desert of Israel's wanderings gives water and manna with God's grace alone to a people who are willing to trust.

The economic rules given in this context were obviously intended for practice in Canaan, not in the desert. Indeed, the Torah's final book, Deuteronomy, is filled with warnings about how easy it will be, once one has become too comfortably settled in the land, to forget that all of life's bounty is divine gift, rather than merited reward due human labor (e.g., Deut. 6:10-12; 8). Much of Deuteronomy was almost certainly written in retrospect, long after Israel had abandoned its heritage via its failed flirtation with monarchy. Its purpose in part was to remind the returning exiles of the original heritage of socioeconomic principles for living that remained Israel's gift from God.

The core of that heritage was the collection of economic provisions that set Israel apart from all other nations. Scholars have frequently pointed out the generally similar premise underlying both YHWH's covenant with Israel and other nations' kings' relationship with the people. YHWH the king provides true peace and security, and, in exchange, the people give honor and loyalty to King YHWH alone. But within this familiar framework was a subversive distinction. While other nations looked to human kings and their "military-industrial complexes" for security and justice, Israel was to depend completely on the bounty and justice of the unseen God as experienced in the local household/clan-based social economy. One of the practical implications of this distinction was that rather than expecting the human king to provide justice for the weaker members of society (traditionally referred to as "widows, orphans, and sojourners"), YHWH put this responsibility directly into the hands of the people as a congregation/*ekklēsia*. For instance,

> Every third year you shall bring out the full tithe of your produce for that year, and store it within your towns; the Levites, because they have no allotment or inheritance with you, as well as the resident aliens, the orphans, and the widows in your towns, may come and eat their fill so that YHWH your God may bless you in all the work that you undertake. (Deut. 14:28-29)

Implicit in this passage and many others is the principle that Israel's religious and practical health as a people is a direct function of how it treats those who are unable to survive without the help of local communities. In a world of high infant and maternal mortality, chronic shortages of food and water and with absolutely no institutional "safety net," such provisions were literally matters of life and death.

Furthermore, Israel was not to trade or make pacts with the Canaanite peoples of the land (e.g., Deut. 7:1-6). While the Torah announces this principle in religious terms, there is an important economic substrate. What was the main, tempting invitation that led so much of Israel over the centuries to "worship the Ba°als and the Astartes," the gods and goddesses of the indigenous peoples? Was it, as in our world, a matter of more attractive liturgies or more comforting prayers? Hardly was this the case. A look at the worship provisions given in Torah and the collection of prayers and songs contained in the Psalter reveal a rich and powerful set of rituals designed to remind people in exciting and memorable ways of YHWH's saving deeds and powerful faithfulness to the people. Rather, it was the *temptation to return to the "fleshpots" of empire* and thus to abandon YHWH's call to live in sometimes difficult, socioeconomic equality apart from the ways of the Canaanites. Nostalgic memories of life in Egypt play as much to the people's later experience of their Canaanite neighbors' seemingly more bountiful valley harvests in comparison with Israel's hillside pickings:

> We remember the fish we used to eat in Egypt for nothing, the cucumbers, the melons, the leeks, the onions, and the garlic; but now our strength is dried up, and there is nothing at all but this manna to look at. (Num. 11:5-6; cf. Exod. 16:3).

The prophets constantly reminded the people of the price at which this imperial bounty was provided: slavery for the many and wealth for the elite few. The temptation was strong, though, leading not only to constant turning to the Canaanites and to Egypt for provisions (e.g., Gen. 12:10-20; 42:1-4), but eventually to Israel's own monarchy. It should come as no surprise to hear how the prophet Samuel presents God's prediction of what life will be like under a king:

> He said, "These will be the ways of the king who will reign over you: he will take your sons and appoint them to his chariots and to be his horsemen, and to run before his chariots; and he will appoint for himself commanders of thousands and commanders of fifties, and some to plow his ground and to reap his harvest, and to make his implements of war and the equipment of his chariots. He will take your daughters to be perfumers and cooks and bakers. He will take the best of your fields and vineyards and olive orchards and give them to his courtiers. He will take one-tenth of your grain and of your vineyards and give it to his officers and his courtiers. He will take your male and female slaves, and the best of your cattle and donkeys, and put them to his work. He will take one-tenth of your flocks, and you shall be his slaves. And in that day you will cry out because of your king, whom you have chosen for yourselves; but YHWH will not answer you in that day." (1 Sam. 8:11-18)

The operative royal verb is *take*: sons and daughters; fields, vineyards, and orchards; slaves and animals; even freedom itself (cf. Gen. 47:13-25). Note how one of the basic results of monarchy in this description is the breakup of local kinship-based economics, as the labor of sons and daughters is transferred from the local to the imperial sphere. The most extreme example of this was under Solomon's regime, where traditional tribal boundaries were replaced by administrative taxation districts (1 Kgs. 4:7-19). Indeed, despite his fame, a close reading of the biblical narrative shows that the great King Solomon's royal behavior bears a striking resemblance to Pharaoh's (1 Kgs. 4; 9:10-28; 12:1-11). Thus, the entire monarchical experiment is seen as a betrayal of the covenant, which called for trust in YHWH, not human kings, as the securer of economic sustenance. In other words, life was to be experienced at the local social and economic level of extended household and clan, rather than through the centralized economics of empire.

Even within the covenanted life, the Israelites knew that circumstances could be unfair. Accidents of unequal rainfall, illness, or other vicissitudes of life could make some folks relatively wealthier than others. Over time, this could lead, as we well know in our world, to the charging of interest and the concomitant spiraling of debt out of which it can become almost impossible to emerge. Israel's inheritance promised sufficient land upon which each household and clan could make a living that would give "vine and fig tree" for everyone (e.g., Deut. 8:7-10; Mic. 4:3-4; Zech. 3:10). But debt could and did lead to loss of this land for many and the transformation of interdependent farmers and shepherds into landless beggars and slaves.

To remedy this inevitable situation, Israel understood the covenant to provide for periodic relief in the form of the sabbatical and jubilee years. With the advent and passing of the year 2000, much good work has been done in recent years to draw attention to this tradition. Advocates of jubilee have worked for debt relief among the world's poor nations, while proponents of sabbath have focused on restoring a sense of rhythm between work and rest in our often manic, production-oriented society. But neither Jesus nor the New Testament writers thought of these traditions as emergency measures aimed at overcoming centuries of injustice and oppression, but rather as divinely instituted aspects of the everyday pattern of covenant economic relationships among humans and between humans and the earth and its creatures. Let's take a brief look at the context of these provisions in the life of Israel before considering the role they played in the economic life of the *ekklēsia*.

The basic grounding of Israel's understanding of life's economic rhythms is expressed in the first chapter of the Hebrew Scriptures. There we see the familiar narration of God's six days of work and affirmation of that work, followed by the grand pronouncement:

> And on the seventh day God finished the work that he had done, and he rested on the seventh day from all the work that he had done. So God blessed the seventh day and hallowed it, because on it God rested from all the work that he had done in creation. (Gen. 2:2-3)

One could spend enormously fruitful meditation time considering the implications of this statement: *God rested*. The Creator, the One Who Is, *stopped working* and blessed the seventh day. Furthermore, we are told, God *hallowed* that day, the only "hallowing" described in Genesis. As God has hallowed it, so too are the people of God to hallow the sabbath (Exod. 20:8-11; 31:13-17; Deut. 5:12-15). This hallowing means to treat the day as one would any sacred object, place or person: with deep reverence and awe. One daily cycle out of seven, then, was to be given over to "nothing more" than standing in prayerful awe and thanksgiving for the gift of life itself.

This commandment was not intended simply to call people to pious activity, but to ensure that life would not become an endless cycle of production and consumption. For Israelites struggling to make ends meet in the highlands of Canaan, this was a powerful call to *imitate God* by resting from labor on a regular basis. By practicing sabbath, Israel would not only gain refreshment, but it would remember who it was, a people called by God out of empire to live according to a divinely given covenant.

The sabbath alone, of course, could not make up for annual inequalities in rainfall, let alone life-changing inequalities such as injury or disease. To restore the balance of such longer-term inequities, the Torah called for more dramatic measures: the septennial sabbatical year and the even more powerful septennial of septennials, the jubilee year. The key text is Leviticus 25. God calls for a sabbatical *for the earth*. As the Israelites get one day a week to rest, so the earth itself gets a full year of rest once every seven. And then, after seven cycles of this pattern, there is to be announced the great "homebringing," the literal meaning of the Hebrew from which we get the term "jubilee." Not only shall there be no farming that year, but,

> You shall hallow the fiftieth year and you shall proclaim liberty throughout the land to all its inhabitants. You shall return, every one of you, to your property [Hebrew *achuz-zah*] and every one of you to your clan. (Lev. 25:10)

God tells them, in effect: "the great Monopoly game of life may be interesting to play for a while, but every second or third generation at most, everyone goes back to 'Go,' gets $200 and the game starts over." The jubilee calls not only for a rest and for debt relief but for an utterly fresh economic start for everyone. The Hebrew term translated "property" refers to God's solemn promise to Abraham and the Israelites that the Promised Land will be theirs to occupy (Gen. 17:18; Deut. 32:49). However, the gift of land comes with the reminder that the land "shall not be sold in perpetuity, for the land is mine; with me you are but aliens and tenants" (Lev. 25:23). Thus, the jubilee is intended to undergird an economic system which recognizes that *all is divine gift*. There can be no divinely approved inequalities in wealth for the long haul. It is God's will for each member of the people to experience life as bountiful, abundant, filled with the created things that God has declared "good."

The details of the economic system described in the Torah and remembered by the prophets flow out of this most basic principle. For instance, Leviticus 19 forbids the reaping of the harvest to the edges of the field, so that the poor can always find sustenance. Further, it prohibits such basic economic injustices as theft, fraud, and withholding of a worker's wages. The jubilee chapter continues by prohibiting the taking of interest or making a profit from the economic difficulties of one's own kin (Lev. 25:35-37). Numerous other provisions are given to fill in some of the day-to-day details of what it means to structure a community's economic life around a shared covenant with the Creator.

We should recognize that Israel well knew the difficulty of living out such a system of covenant economics. The very fact that the Torah contains so many details is evidence that the practical means of living covenant were not so obvious or easy that they did not require being enshrined in a sacred text. Similarly, we see how centuries of prophetic critique focused its wrath on the elite of Israel, who obtained comfort and wealth at the expense of their less fortunate sisters and brothers. A key example of such a text is one from Ezekiel which sheds light on an otherwise misinterpreted tradition:

> This was the guilt of your sister Sodom: she and her daughters had pride, excess of food, and prosperous ease, but did not aid the poor and needy. (Ezek. 16:49)

From the prophet's perspective, the sin of Sodom had nothing to do with sexuality and everything to do with economics: unwillingness to share their abundance with those in need. Seemingly countless prophetic passages echo Ezekiel's sentiment, lamenting the selfishness and greed of the wealthy. Yet, despite this constant injustice, Israel never engaged in the even worse sin of denying the terms of the covenant itself (cf. Mark 3:28-29). That the prophets' harsh critiques were acknowledged as God's Word showed that even those targeted by the prophets knew the truth of their word.

"Sell What You Have": *Covenant Economics in the* Ekklēsia

Both the framework of covenant economics and the prophetic memory of the difficulty of living by its terms were familiar to Jesus and his disciples. Thus, in considering how the *ekklēsia* should shape its own economic life, the New Testament writers turned first to this biblical tradition.

A central challenge for translating the biblical tradition of economic equality into the life of the *ekklēsia* was the difference between Israel as a community largely of village-based farmers and the later discipleship communities as city dwellers living amidst an imperial economy. Jesus' unrelenting critique of the wealthy found in the Gospels was grounded in the "limited good" economic perspective of Palestinian peasants. Within that perspective, economic life is seen as finite and bounded: for one person to become wealthier necessarily means someone else is becoming poorer. Such a change in the status quo is understood as expressing disdain for one's neighbors and thus as contrary to Torah, since a rich person must be willing to become so at the expense of his or her sisters and brothers, from whom the new wealth must have been taken one way or another. This idea of limited good is, of course, totally contrary to the dominant economic worldview of free market capitalism in our time, which (falsely) envisions the economic realm as an "expanding pie" in which all participants can receive larger and larger shares. But in the first-century Mediterranean, the idea that the economy could continue to "grow" forever was unimaginable. Not surprisingly, therefore, peasants felt a basic resentment toward the wealthy, yet felt generally powerless to do anything about it. This was all the more true in a situation where the inequality was made worse by Roman policies that enhanced the wealth-making opportunities of the indigenous elite in exchange for their loyalty to the empire. The most extreme example of this was Herod, whose fabulous, ostentatious building projects were seen by the Jerusalem poor not as "public works" but as part of a shameless self-promotion scheme on the part of a half-Jewish, Roman collaborator.

Jesus, of course, railed frequently against the rich generally and people like Herod and the Jerusalem elite specifically for hypocritically parading around in fancy clothes while pretending to care about the ordinary person's welfare (e.g., Luke 6:24-25; Mark 12:38-44; Matt. 24:27-28). He noted famously the greater likelihood of a camel passing through the eye of a needle than for a rich person to enter the reign of God (Mark 10:23-28; Luke 18:24-

27; Matt. 19:23-26). He urged his disciples not to be distracted by the pursuit of wealth, warning that it would become a fatal distraction from one's participation in God's reign (Matt. 6:24; Luke 16:13). But other than making the poor feel momentarily better by seeing the rich ridiculed, how would these teachings help transform the terrible economic inequalities of the time into a world governed by covenant and jubilee principles?

The Gospels show Jesus offering two further teachings on wealth that were the basis for the urban *ekklēsiai*'s own economic practices. First, those with wealth *must* sell all their possessions and give them to the poor, to whom they truly belong (e.g., Mark 10:17-22; Luke 12:33-34; 19:1-10). This difficult saying has been avoided and spiritualized by generations of interpreters attached to their own wealth, but it could not be said more clearly nor more emphatically than it is in the Gospels. For reasons we will see shortly, Luke among the evangelists is most insistent on the absolute nature of this condition: "None of you can become my disciple if you do not give up all your possessions" (Luke 14:33).

The second teaching was that the discipleship community must *model* covenant economics in its own life (e.g., Mark 10:28-30). The petition in the Lord's Prayer to "forgive us our debts as we forgive those in debt to us" (Matt. 6:12) refers primarily not to grudges against personal slights but explicitly to economic obligations, which are to be forgiven according to the jubilee command. Of course, such a principle flows clearly from the social relationships noted earlier in this chapter: to consider members of the *ekklēsia* as one's sisters and brothers is to practice economics based on the other's need for sustenance rather than one's own desire for profit or luxury. Only a most callous and selfish individual would see one's family member's economic misfortune as an opportunity for one's own gain by, for example, charging interest or taking one's land as collateral for a loan. Becoming and remaining a disciple of Jesus was intended, therefore, to pull one into an *ekklēsia* in which economic relationships were based on *kinship* rather than *kingship*.

This brings us back to the question, How could this be done in a city environment suffused with imperial economy? Luke's second volume, Acts, along with Revelation—both directed to urban audiences—provide much guidance.

Luke insists so strongly on narrating Jesus' uncompromising command about shedding one's attachment to wealth because he well understood how the first step in living the economic call of the *ekklēsia* was to transform people's perceptions that the world was dominated by scarcity rather than abundance. For the teeming masses of poor people in places such as Ephesus, wealth seemed impossibly far away. The patronage system put the poor so many rungs down the ladder from the elite that there seemed to be no way to get access to the mountains of treasure enjoyed by the rich. Thus, in daily life, one struggled not to "rise up the ladder" as one might aspire to in our society, but simply to garner food and shelter for today. As a result, most people's primary perception was that food and other necessities were inherently scarce. This was exacerbated, of course, by the imperial religious propaganda that endorsed the status quo as the divinely established economic and social order. No use dreaming or working for things to be different; to do so was to seek to upset the divine balance.

Luke's two volumes systematically rip the cover off this lie. Beginning with Mary's Magnificat (Luke 1:46-65) and continuing through John the Baptist's expression of the meaning of *metanoia*/repentance (Luke 3:7-14), Luke's Gospel calls its audience, filled with well-educated and prosperous urban people, to use their economic power to begin the practice of jubilee. The Lucan paradigm of this repentance is Zacchaeus, the tax collector who vows to pay back fourfold what he has gained by fraud and to give half of his possessions to the poor (Luke 19:1-10). If a hated and avaricious tax collector can do it, Luke's Jesus suggests, then anyone can and should! Thus, Luke appeals to his listeners to make a radical break with the unjust status quo and allow the poor to experience life from a new perspective, one in which God's abundance, rather than imperially controlled scarcity, is the order of the day.

If Luke's Gospel announces, then illustrates Jesus' first teaching about jubilee economics beginning with the repentance of the wealthy, his second volume shows how the *ekklēsia* is to live jubilee within its own economic relationships. Just as the Gospel began with the outpouring of the Holy Spirit on John the Baptist and on Mary, so Acts begins with the outpouring of the Spirit on the newly formed *ekklēsia* in Jerusalem on the feast of Pentecost. And as that Spirit led both John and Mary to call for the redistribution of the abundance held by the few into the hands of the many, so that same Spirit leads the disciples to express their repentance in the most practical of terms:

> All who believed were together and had all things in common; they would sell their possessions and goods and distribute the proceeds to all, as any had need. (Acts 2:44-45)

> Now the whole group of those who believed were of one heart and soul, and no one claimed private ownership of any possessions, but everything they owned was held in common. With great power the apostles gave their testimony to the resurrection of the Lord Jesus, and great grace was upon them all. There was not a needy person among them, for as many as owned lands or houses sold them and brought the proceeds of what was sold. They laid it at the apostles' feet, and it was distributed to each as any had need. (Acts 4:32-35)

These oft-quoted passages are sometimes written off by interpreters who refuse to take seriously the key role economics played in the life of the first *ekklēsia*. But when read both in the context of Hebrew Scriptures and of Luke's two-volume work, there is no doubt that Luke understood the sharing of material goods within the *ekklēsia* to be the central, concrete expression of one's trust in the Way of Jesus. For example, in the subsequent story in Acts 5, a couple named Ananias and Sapphira sell a piece of property but then embezzle (5:2 [Greek *enosphisato*]; cf. Titus 2:10) some of the proceeds before depositing the remainder at the apostles' feet.

Peter challenges Ananias not for being greedy but for lying to the Holy Spirit, that is, pretending to make a full commitment to the *ekklēsia*. Acts will not allow for wealthy persons to feign discipleship while maintaining security in the world's unjust economic system. To be the *ekklēsia*, all members must be willing to trust that the Spirit is guiding them as a new family who in turn trust one another. The pragmatic (cf. Acts 5:4 [*pragma*]) test of this trust is *economic*. To say one has faith in God while storing up worldly treasures that truly belong to the poor is to lie to the Holy Spirit.

If Luke's perspective on these questions represented a New Testament anomaly, one might write it off, as have some scholars, as a failed dream of a radical minority. But on examining the entire New Testament message on the relationship between economics and the *ekklēsia*, we see that, if anything, Luke's position is "centrist" in relation to that of writers like John of Patmos. Revelation does not appeal to the wealthy to share generously. Instead, it expresses the divine voice calling God's people to "come out" of the imperial economy altogether. Revelation 18 presents this call as a kind of liturgical fire alarm. God knows that the *ekklēsiai* live in "Babylon," a common codeword for the Roman empire. But a closer look at the entire chapter makes clear that John does not understand God to be calling the *ekklēsia* literally to leave town, as the Israelites understood the call to leave Egypt and as did the Jews who left first-century B.C.E. Jerusalem to establish a new community at Qumran in the Judean desert. What they are to "come out" from is explicitly the system of global trade and its inherent exploitation of the poor that Rome claimed to be a gift of the gods. Throughout Revelation 18, we hear the cries of three groups of mourners: "the kings of the earth," "the merchants of the earth," and "all shipmasters and seafarers, sailors and all whose trade is on the sea." They lament not in compassion for Babylon's suffering but for the loss of their own profit-making opportunities, "since no one buys their cargo anymore" (18:11). After this verse comes an incredibly detailed description of that cargo, the "juicy fruits" (18:14 [Greek *hopōra*]) of the imperial economy, from luxury items such as gold and jewels to everyday staples such as flour, oil, and wine. John's apocalyptic insight reveals to him that behind the official propaganda which gives thanks to the gods for all these good things, the one, true God has already condemned a system that is not from God at all but from "the dragon" and the beasts to whom the dragon's power has been given (13:1-17).

The counterpart to the mourners are those who are invited to celebrate this unveiling of empire's economic collapse: "you saints and apostles and prophets" (Rev. 18:20). These are none other than the members of the seven *ekklēsiai* to whom John addresses his letter. They can rejoice not simply in the dark spectacle of Babylon's fall, but in the more light-filled emergence from heaven of God's holy city, New Jerusalem. This city is the opposite of Babylon not because the latter is filled with "goodies" while the former is a stark, monkish retreat. On the contrary, New Jerusalem is just as jewel-filled and abundant as is the fallen, imperial city. Its vision of gold-paved streets suggests a divine abundance which undermines the claims of the imperial economy to be the provider of wealth. The central difference is that Babylon's luxury is the result of the exploitation of the many by the few, while New Jerusalem's treasure is the result of God's creative abundance. Put another way, empire offers "the best that money can buy," while God gives what the *ekklēsia* needs as a free gift.

It can be very difficult for Christians today to understand that John's vision was not a utopian fantasy but a poetic expression of what the daily life of the *ekklēsia* was to be like. One's economic life is an expression of where one's trust truly lies. Regardless of one's stated commitment to Jesus, each act of participation in the imperial economy is a form of uncleanness and, if done with full intentionality, rises to the level of what the Bible calls "sin." This is certainly how John saw it in presenting his picture of the dueling liturgies between "heaven" and "earth" (compare Rev. 7 and 13). Where the Hebrew Scriptures' authors developed a "purity code" grounded in the cleanness or uncleanness of animals, foods or persons (e.g., Gen. 1; Deut. 7), John shares Jesus' view that one's participation in acts that rob people of social dignity and economic sustenance are the truly unclean deeds (cf. Mark 7:1-23).

The way to remain clean, then, was to engage as much as possible only in economic exchanges grounded in covenant and jubilee, in which one saw one's trading partner as a sister or brother. This might well mean that in the transition period during which people gradually withdrew their allegiance to the imperial economy, one might experience a sense of scarcity in a way analogous to that of an addict quitting drugs. Being "deprived" of heroin, nicotine, or television might seem a form of asceticism for a while, but eventually, the restoration of health and opportunity to partake of the many free gifts of which the addict is often oblivious can be experienced as more than making up for the "loss" of the addiction. A similar argument is made by many today who can hardly imagine life outside the global economic empire we are coming to take more and more as "divinely inspired" each day. But all this shows is how similar our world is in this regard to that of the first *ekklēsiai*. They, too, as people enmeshed in city life, could hardly imagine making a go of it apart from Rome's economy. And yet this is clearly what John, bringing forward the Hebrew Scriptures that shape his entire faith perspective, proclaims as God's call to the *ekklēsiai*. Just as the Jerusalem *ekklēsia* in Acts shared all things in common and experienced abundance, so too John reminds his audience in Asia that they are to live as a holy people set apart economically from empire.

While Luke and John of Patmos offer the most sustained reflection on the economic life of the *ekklēsia*, numerous other New Testament writers make briefer comments in support of this basic perspective. For example, Paul, as we have seen, admonishes the elite Corinthians for showing off their wealth-based status in front of their poor and struggling sisters and brothers. Further, he calls the *ekklēsiai* around the Mediterranean to provide economic support to the *ekklēsia* in Jerusalem in time of famine-induced poverty (Rom. 15:25-27; 1 Cor. 16:1-3). Just as individual *ekklēsia* members are to see one another as family, so too the worldwide *ekklēsia* is to be in such a relationship, even if people never actually set eyes on their geographically distant sisters and brothers. The author of the letter of James says that faith that offers only lip service to the sister or brother in economic need is "dead" (Jas. 2:15-17). He then goes on to condemn harshly the rich for putting their security in "gold and silver" while exploiting their laborers (Jas. 5:1-6). And while not speaking directly in economic language, John's Gospel condemns those who choose the "glory" people give one another through wealth and social position over the glory God gives to those joined as branches to the Vine (e.g., John 12:42-43, 15:1-8).

Of all the aspects of early church life, it is the economic radicality of the New Testament message that most Christians in the First World today find most difficult to hear and to practice. We are so deeply steeped in the "gospel" of global trade that to speak of other systems, let alone claim them as God's way, is often seen as heresy of the highest order. And indeed, that is precisely what it is from the perspective of the defenders of empire. From Mesopotamia to Egypt to Babylon to Rome to today's global corporations, proponents of imperial economics have attempted with great success to claim divine approval for their viewpoint. And with equal vigor if less access to mass media, God's prophets, apostles, and saints have proclaimed a totally different economic order as the Way of the Creator. If God's people continue today to find themselves living in Babylon, it remains the divine call to "come out" and make visible an economy in which the celebration of true abundance is at the heart of the matter.

Reflection Questions

1. Consider your own experience of "family." How has your personal family history bonded you and/or alienated you from specific persons, living and dead? What would it mean to you to look upon members of a faith community as "sisters" and "brothers"?

2. Consider basic relational units of your life: those with whom you live, your workplace colleagues, circles of friends or other associates, members of church. On what basis is power distributed—for example: wealth, age, social status, job description, or other formal attributes of "office," and so forth? How would these relationships be different if power were shared equally?

3. In your church tradition or practice, how are power and leadership exercised? What similarities or differences are there between your community's current exercise of power and leadership and that attributed to the early *ekklēsia*?

4. Do you envision life's resources as basically scarce or basically abundant? How has your attitude been formed? How does what you hear preached or see practiced in church reinforce or challenge this attitude?

5. Imagine a discipleship community that was struggling to "come out" of the imperial economy and to live in a covenanted economy. How would you envision getting from here to there? What feelings arise in you as you consider each step on the journey? Do you feel more like someone giving up a cherished practice or someone being released from bondage?

4

Ministry

For many Roman Catholics in the United States today, issues of who engages in ministry often seem like one of the major focal points of church discussion and argument. But like the similarly frequent topic of sexuality, the New Testament says very little on the matter at all. While the previous chapter could draw on a rich, if challenging, tradition of texts to consider the church's social and economic relationships, much of what we can glean from the New Testament about ministry comes through arguments from silence.

For instance, while priests for Catholics and ordained clergy for mainline Protestants have been generally considered the central providers of ministry to the church over the centuries, the New Testament *never* portrays Jesus "ordaining" anyone or "instituting" a priesthood in his name. Only in hindsight can some passages be interpreted as expressing some kind of ordination, such as those in which hands are laid on certain persons to prepare them to go out in service (e.g., Acts 6:6; 8:17; 13:12-13). Such rituals, however, were frequent in many contexts in the ancient world, and the New Testament texts nowhere associate them with "priesthood" or "clergy." The final cycle of New Testament writings shows the emergence of a three-part, "official" ministry of *diakonoi* (servants), *presbyteroi* (elders), and *episkopoi* (overseers) (e.g., 1 Tim. 3:1-13; 5:17). However, to translate these terms both linguistically and socioculturally into the modern terms "deacons," "priests," and "bishops" is to do serious violence to the original contexts of their use in the New Testament, Hebrew Scriptures, and the wider Greco-Roman world. Thus, we must begin our exploration not by attempting to justify later developments or current usage with reference to the New Testament, but by listening with fresh ears to the notions of ministry found in the earliest self-descriptions of the *ekklēsia*. Then we will be able to understand how the three-part ministry was originally intended to function.

Ministry and Leadership in the Hebrew Scriptures

Our first determination must be the bounds of the term "ministry" with reference to the church. While some might define it narrowly to refer to official, sacramental, or other liturgical duties, others use it widely to refer to anything a believer does with a mind and heart focused on serving God and God's people. The Bible does not answer this question for us, since the set of nuances belonging to our English word "ministry" does not correspond directly to any specific Hebrew or Greek term. For example, outside the church, we know that many English-speaking countries have long used this term to refer to a government office, such as the Foreign Ministry. Further, "to minister" is to provide for the needs of someone or some group, regardless of religious motivation or authority, from which we get other everyday, secular terms such as "administer" or "ministrate."

The closest we can get is the Hebrew *sharath*, a word with a wide range of nuances, too. While often designating the service of priests or Levites in the Jerusalem temple or earlier in Israel's history, it also is used to refer to:

- Royal domestic servants (e.g., 1 Kgs. 1:4), government officials (e.g., Prov. 29:12) or official singers (e.g., 1 Chr. 6:31-32)

- Assistants to other important persons (e.g., Joshua to Moses, Exod. 24:13)

- Any person serving God, whether or not a priest (e.g., foreigners, Isa. 56:6; the "blameless," Ps. 101:6)

- Metaphorically of creation serving God (e.g., fire and flame, Ps. 104:4; rams, Isa. 60:7)

While some of these categories correspond to our sense of "ministry" as work performed in an explicitly religious context, others conceive of ministry as political or even menial service to a person in power or authority. Of course, the distinction between service in the realm of "religion" as separate from the realm of "politics" is one largely unknown until recent centuries. Rather, one might have distinguished what we call "cultic" activities from noncultic. Rather than get caught up in arguing over these categories, we will consider under the rubric "ministry" any service to the faith community that is performed with a religious motivation, that is, as ultimately in service to God. Thus, whether a particular act qualifies as "ministry" is a matter not of *function* but of *intention*. For instance, in our society, "secular" occupations such as carpentry, health care, or law are not normally thought of as "religious" vocations. However, when the person engaged in such a pursuit is doing so out of a sense of divine call to serve the community through a God-given talent or ability, it can be considered to be "ministry." This distinction is the result not of a modern redefinition of a traditionally more narrow term but of recovering the sense of it understood first by Israel and then by the *ekklēsia*.

Israel's stories of its earliest experience as a people did not, of course, include a developed religious institution. The household narratives of Genesis show the patriarchs building altars, making vows, and encountering God in dreams and visions, but rarely portray activities that we might think of as ministry. But with the Exodus narrative, we see for the first time *leadership* functions that extend beyond the household or clan: Moses and Aaron become leaders of a holy nation in relation to a group called "the elders of Israel." In the narratives of the wilderness journeying, leadership consists mostly in keeping the people faithful to the task of becoming the people of YHWH by trusting in YHWH's exclusive sovereignty over their lives, both individually and collectively. Numerous stories of grumbling, recalcitrance, and outright rebellion show Moses and Aaron taking harsh steps to maintain loyalty, including the apparent mass slaughter of resisters (e.g., Num. 16).

Their authority as named individuals with strong (if deeply flawed) personalities often stands against the more collective authority of "the elders of Israel" (Hebrew *ziqnei yisrael;* Greek *gerousia huiōn Israel*). The Hebrew term *zaqen* literally means "bearded" and was a euphemism for male elders. In the ancient world, as in most tribal societies across the millennia, to live to old age was a sign both of divine favor and of a wisdom gained from long years of experience. The Greek term *gerousia* reflects a very similar concept found in Hellenistic cultures. But it is not a specific elder whose wisdom is respected, but the *community of elders acting as a body.* A key incident showing the importance of this collective authority is found in Numbers 11. After yet another episode in which the people grumble against the whole Exodus project, recalling with salivating mouths the "bounty" of Egypt, Moses reaches the breaking point and cries to God that he is about to quit. YHWH strengthens him by saying:

> Gather for me seventy of the elders of Israel, whom you know to be the elders of the people and officers [Hebrew *shoter*] over them; bring them to the tent of meeting, and have them take their place there with you. I will come down and talk with you there; and I will take some of the spirit that is on you and put it on them; and they shall bear the burden of the people along with you so that you will not bear it all by yourself. (Num. 11:16-17)

Moses recounts this incident to the people in his departure speech on the edge of the Land, but claims the idea for himself rather than as YHWH's command and also replaces the figure of "the elders of Israel" with tribal leaders:

> Choose for each of your tribes individuals who are wise, discerning, and reputable to be your leaders. "You answered me, 'The plan you have proposed is a good one.'" So I took the leaders of your tribes, wise and reputable individuals, and installed them as leaders over you, commanders [Hebrew *sar*] of thousands, commanders of hundreds, commanders of fifties, commanders of tens, and officials [Hebrew *shoter*], throughout your tribes. (Deut. 1:13-15)

Note how God's command in Numbers involved sharing out some of YHWH's own spirit among the people, whereas Moses' (or the Deuteronomist's) revised version offers simply a distribution of authority down to the most local units, with no guarantee of YHWH's approval or inspiration.

The difference in versions may also reflect two different biblical authors in later times with different views on how human and divine authority interact. But whether we see the struggle as between later authors or as a historical event does not change the fact that Israel's memory included powerful stories of how difficult it was to establish a line between acceptance of a human leader as God's spokesperson for a given moment and more generally equating human authority with divine authority. One might argue that the entire history of Israel's journey between Exodus and exile is a story of this struggle, with heroic "judges" like Gideon adamantly rejecting the people's attempt to make him an absolute ruler (Judg. 6-8, esp. 8:22-23) and others like Saul or Solomon reveling in human power and adulation while enriching themselves in the process.

Thus, we see established from the beginning a dynamic tension between three sources of power: God, groups of elders and officials, and powerful individuals. For the period covering the Exodus and the early generations in the Land (Joshua and Judges), this tension seems to have been maintained in ways that allowed the Israelites to maintain a healthy balance between order and chaos. Leadership in the household/clan would probably have been exercised by a local council of elders, with the role of charismatic "judges" reserved for times of external threat of violence. However, with the establishment of the monarchy, the biblical writers show Israel succumbing to the temptation to be "like other nations" (1 Sam. 8:5, 20). It is at this stage that Israel must deal with the problem of *inherited* power rather than power grounded in God's Spirit and election. It is also the period in which what we most easily associate with "ministry" begins to be practiced: the system of sacrifices and other religious rituals organized around the Jerusalem Temple and priesthood. From a series of charismatic leaders (e.g., Moses, Joshua, the judges) in tension with a council of elders, Israel's authority structure is transformed into a system of royal officials and priests in tension with *prophets*. The story of the monarchy is adamant in its view that none of these roles is to be passed from generation to generation as one passes property or land. The priest Eli's sons are "worthless," taking the juiciest portions of the sacrifice for themselves (1 Sam. 2:12-17). The prophet Samuel's sons, whom he appoints as judges, similarly are described as taking bribes and "perverting justice" (1 Sam. 8:1-3). Indeed, it is their behavior that leads the elders of Israel to cry out to Samuel for a king. Finally, although there is no fault found with the sons of the first king, Saul, his successor David's sons are shown in detail to be violent, greedy, and power-seeking, including the "hero" son Solomon, whom the author of First Kings portrays first as an Israelite pharaoh and then as the leading idolater in all of Israel's history (1 Kgs. 9:15-21; 10:14-29; 11:1-10). Solomon's own son is such a tyrant that the northern tribes flee from his rule (1 Kgs. 12:1-19).

Yet, according to the Torah received by Moses long before the monarchy, the priesthood was to be the inheritance of the tribe of Levi, given to them in place of a piece of the Land. Scholars who have looked closely at this apparent paradox have shown clearly that the Hebrew Scriptures reflect at least two views of priestly authority. One, given expression in the Deuteronomistic History and in the prophetic tradition of Jeremiah, saw priesthood as inherently linked with *prophecy*, that is, the inspired utterance of God's Word. It is a tradition rooted in Moses' claim that God will "raise up for you a prophet like me from among your own people" (Deut. 18:15-18). For this tradition, Moses is the paradigm of priest and prophet: the one who both mediates the sacred for the people *and* becomes God's mouthpiece. Its formal lineage began with David's priest, Abiathar, but may well go back to premonarchic practices at local shrines throughout Canaan. This priest was rejected by Solomon because of Abiathar's siding with David's son Adonijah against Solomon during the struggle for succession (2 Sam. 15:24-35; 1 Kgs. 1:7; 2:26-27). Solomon banished Abiathar to the town of Anathoth just outside Jerusalem, where Jeremiah lived some three hundred years later among a community of exiled priests (Jer. 1:1). From this position just outside the circles of power yet with a strong memory and experience of divine inspiration, Jeremiah and his community sought to maintain the tradition of a prophetic priesthood totally dependent on God rather than a human grant of authority.

The second tradition grounded priesthood in the status of *the Temple* as God's holy abode. Narratives expressing this view are often referred to by scholars as coming from the pen of the "Priestly" writer, the author of, among other texts, the ritual legislation found in Exodus and Leviticus. These people also rooted their tradition in two sources: Aaron as priest, of coequal importance to Moses, and Zadok, David's and Solomon's priest whose lineage continued down to the Sadducees of Jesus' time (Aaron: Exod. 19:24; 28:1-4; 29:5-9; Zadok: 2 Sam. 8:17; 1 Kgs. 1:8; 2:35). It was this tradition that was claimed by Ezra, the leader of those returning from Babylonian exile to rebuild the Temple and to restore its priesthood (Ezra 7:1-6). Within this tradition, Israel's holiness, both collectively and among the people as individuals, was mediated by the sacrificial system carried out by the Jerusalem priesthood. While this segment of Israel's population managed to gain and hold onto power for hundreds of years, it was frequently challenged by prophetic voices who insisted that

Israel's holiness was a matter of moral, not ritual practice (e.g., Mic. 6:1-8; Isa. 58). Micah contrasted the absurdity of "thousands of rams, with ten thousands of rivers of oil" with what YHWH truly requires: "to do justice, and to love kindness, and to walk humbly with your God." The author of Isaiah 58 challenged the ritual fasting led by Ezra's postexilic priesthood by reminding them that true fasting involved housing the homeless and sharing bread with the hungry. Both during and after the monarchy, then, Israel's practice of ministry included a dynamic—sometimes outright hostile—tension between a hereditary, centralized priesthood imbued with official authority and prophets from the margins of "respectable society" who claimed nothing more nor less than to have been chosen by God to speak a truth that called Israel back to its covenant commitment.

In the five hundred plus years from the time of Ezra to the time of Jesus, Israel's experience of the tension between royal and prophetic bases for priesthood was complicated by the fact of foreign imperial control. First Persia, then Greece, and finally Rome controlled the political and hence, the religious authority of Israel's leaders. It was one thing to engage in the internal struggle between Israel's own monarchical establishment and its prophetic memory of the powerful God unconfined by human systems of power, and another when the establishment was an oppressive foreign government. Some priests and royal officials took for themselves and advocated for others the path of "realpolitik," an acknowledgment that Jerusalem's priestly authority was held subject to colonial consent. Others, though, interpreted the situation as calling for a renewed commitment to the covenant between the people of Israel and YHWH alone, which necessarily called for resistance to imperial authority. Over the centuries, this conflict was expressed periodically in word and deed, from prophetic denunciations of the leadership's "sellout" to empire to popular movements of violent and nonviolent protest.

The struggle peaked during and just after the reign of Herod as king of Judea. Jerusalem's priests and scribes saw the half-Jewish, self-aggrandizing Herod as a necessary evil, a Roman puppet who needed to be tolerated to allow the Temple system of sacrifice and priestly power to continue. Others saw it as the ultimate betrayal of Israel's history and tradition. Jesus' own ministry took place amidst this terrible time, when popular prophets and messianic figures roamed town and countryside seeking to organize the people into rebellion against Herod and Rome. A generation after Jesus, there *was* a rebellion, culminating in the Roman destruction of Jerusalem and its priesthood in 70 C.E. While this ideological and physical battle was raging in Palestine, though, communities of Jesus' followers were left wondering how to shape the ministry of their own *ekklēsiai*.

Service, Leadership, and Divine Mediation in the Ekklēsia

In the cities far removed from the nationalistic cauldron of Jerusalem, Jews and Gentiles were coming together as a new manifestation of "God's people." We have seen how the social and economic structure of patronage shaped relationships within the dominant culture, presenting authority and power in a "trickle-down" pyramid. At the same time, we have seen how Paul's proclamation of "in Christ Jesus, no slave or free" implied rejection of such a system in favor of a more egalitarian distribution of authority grounded in the gifts of the Holy Spirit distributed as the Spirit, not a social elite, saw fit. We have also seen that the formal rituals familiar to Christians today were as yet unknown in the first generations of the *ekklēsia*. What did "ministry" mean in these cities and in this context, given both Israel's experience and the Greco-Roman culture in which the *ekklēsia* was immersed?

The Gospels do not provide much in the way of specifics to which the *ekklēsia* could turn in considering this question. On the one hand, this reflects the great difference in emphasis between the early *ekklēsia* and the church today on what the most pressing questions were. In the relative comfort and privilege of middle-class America and western Europe, Christians can afford to take the time to argue over such issues as women clergy, the relationships between the ordained and lay, and the minutiae of ministerial functions. In the first decades of discipleship, however, just as in Latin American, Asian, or African contexts today, more basic matters such as sheer survival and faith amidst grinding poverty, disease, and oppression necessarily took precedence. We must keep in mind this difference in context as we look at what the New Testament says and doesn't say about ministry.

Jesus appears to have focused on a single criterion for ministry: those who wish to have authority in the *ekklēsia* must be servants of all (e.g., Mark 10:35-45). The Gospels portray a constant grasping for power among Jesus' disciples, understandable within the world around them, but completely contrary to the Way Jesus was trying to inculcate. But just as Jesus had no "credentials" to back up his Way apart from the claim that it was *God's* Way, the disciples after Easter could claim no official authority to legitimate their actions. The *ekklēsia*, on the margins of both the synagogue and the wider society, had to fend for itself in shaping its own relationships of power and authority. The criterion of *servant leadership* would be the foundational principle upon which all other decisions would be evaluated.

Similarly, both Paul's teachings and his personal example consistently embody this tradition. He repeatedly emphasizes his own lack of social standing, indeed, he experiences the abuse as a constant and expected companion. In attempting to challenge the Corinthians who are trying to succeed at the local game of power grabbing, he tells them with evident sarcasm:

> We are fools for the sake of Christ, but you are wise in Christ. We are weak, but you are strong. You are held in honor, but we in disrepute. To the present hour we are hungry and thirsty, we are poorly clothed and beaten and homeless, and we grow weary from the work of our own hands. When reviled, we bless; when persecuted, we endure; when slandered, we speak kindly. We have become like the rubbish

of the world, the dregs of all things, to this very day. (1 Cor. 4:10-13; cf. 2 Cor. 6:3-10; 11:14-30)

For Paul, such treatment was not, however, the bitter pill it might seem to us, but the joy of living in the freedom of utter dependence on God for everything. Like penniless pilgrims over the centuries, Paul knew and proclaimed that ridding oneself of the need for human approval was an exhilarating and truly empowering act of graced freedom. The ministry he exercised and called for within the *ekklēsia* stemmed from this central awareness, from his understanding of the power of the cross of Jesus.

At the same time, Paul absolutely insisted on his status as an *apostle*. This status was a matter not of office or worldly prestige but of its literal meaning of "one sent forth." His experience of the risen Jesus transformed his own sense of ministry from zealous guardian of Pharasaic orthodoxy to tireless missionary to the world. He most adamantly was willing to criticize those for whom the title apostle was becoming a claim to honor within the *ekklēsia*. For instance, he contrasts his own ministry with others who have been influencing the Corinthians contrary to Paul's own teaching and example:

Therefore I am content with weaknesses, insults, hardships, persecutions, and calamities for the sake of Christ; for whenever I am weak, then I am strong. I have been a fool! You forced me to it. Indeed you should have been the ones commending me, for I am not at all inferior to these super-apostles, even though I am nothing. The signs of a true apostle were performed among you with utmost patience, signs and wonders and mighty works. (2 Cor. 12:10-12)

The "signs of a true apostle" are the very willingness to experi-ence the insults, hardships, and so forth, to which he has been subject. The sarcastically labeled "superapostles" apparently sought to become important figures because of their position. Paul similarly shows his disdain for "the so-called pillars" of the *ekklēsia* in Jerusalem: James, Cephas, and John (Gal. 2:6-9).

This contrast between "apostle" as an emerging office of leadership and as a functional description of one's "having been sent" is found also in John's Gospel, where the Greek verb *apostellō*, "to be sent," is used twenty-eight times, while the noun *apostolos* is used but once, and even there in a functional sense (John 13:16). Jesus is "the one sent" *par excellence*, and he sends his disciples out just as God has sent him (John 20:21). The Gospel's closing scene, in which Jesus three times asks Peter about his love for Jesus, culminates not in Jesus' granting Peter primacy over others, but in commanding him to be a shepherd who loves and cares for the sheep to the point of being willing to lay down his life for them if necessary (21:15-19). There can be little doubt that the *ekklēsia*'s earliest understanding of its ministry was grounded in these traditions and principles.

But in the Greco-Roman cities, such notions would be seen as totally subversive. In addition to the "divinely inspired" patronage structure, the Stoic philosophy widely popular among the educated provided an explicit, theoretical underpinning for ministerial hierarchy. A central social metaphor for Stoics was that of the human body, in which each part had its place. Some body parts (people) were destined by "nature" to be in control and esteemed, while others were assigned lowlier roles, which should be accepted as the proper order of things. In one of his most famous images, Paul meets the Stoic ideal head-on (1 Cor. 12:12-27). Although the body (of Christ) which is the *ekklēsia* indeed has many differentiated parts, they are to function in complete interdependence with one another. In reshaping the Stoic image, he confronts both the arrogance of the "important" parts and the low self-esteem of the "lesser" parts. God, through the energizing power of the Holy Spirit, has arranged the parts of Christ's ecclesial body, not human beings. If all are one in the same Spirit, Paul insists, the important "eye" or "head" cannot feel superior to the "hand" or "feet." Rather than seeing ministry as a means to climb a social ladder of respectability or a means for wielding power over "the weak," he presents it as a diversity of functions acting together for the common good of the whole community.

In this same context, Paul names several specific ministerial functions. It is important to see what he names and what he leaves out. First, he names the variety of gifts (Greek *charismata*), services (Greek *diakoniai*), and activities (Greek *energemata*) given by the Spirit, without distinguishing which Spirit-given aspect falls in each category (12:4-10):

> words of wisdom
> words of knowledge
> faith
> gifts of healing
> powerful works
> prophecy
> discernment of spirits
> tongues (Greek *glossalalia*)
> interpretation of tongues

Then, after he presents his metaphor of the body, he offers another series, this time focused more on function, but overlapping with the first list in part:

> apostles
> prophets
> teachers
> powerful works
> gifts of healing
> helpers
> guidance or leadership (Greek, *kybernēsis*)
> kinds of tongues

All of these gifts and functions not only are to be exercised in coordination for the common good, but are to be always grounded in *love*, a point to which Paul devotes an entire chapter (1 Cor. 13) before continuing with the question of specific ministries. He does not spell out the details of these various ministries because his concern is solely to make sure that *all* ministry is used for the building up of the *ekklēsia* rather than the status of the minister (14:1-33).

Given both the history of Israel and church practice today, one might be struck by a particular ministry of which Paul says nothing at all: priesthood. Outside the context of the Jerusalem Temple, priesthood was practiced not by Jews or followers of Jesus but by officials of the imperial cult and the cults of local deities such as Artemis and Isis. In the imperial cult in particular—that is, the system of ritual in which honor was given to the Roman empire and its highest human representatives—priesthood was a high honor reserved for "friends" of the elite. To be the one to lead the sacrifices that enshrouded the empire in divine authority was to be among those at the pinnacles of power. But for the *ekklēsia*, there was no need for such a system. Paul is adamant that for the discipleship community, the levitical system of animal sacrifice has been rendered obsolete, even before the actual destruction of the Temple subsequent to Paul's years of ministry. The people's commitment to live Torah's call to covenant justice and right-eousness was no longer to be ratified through the ritual intervention of a priest, but simply by God's gift of grace. And given the utter rejection of the hierarchical Roman social and economic system, there was certainly no inclination to replicate in the *ekklēsia* the practices of the imperial and local cults.

The Greek word for priest, *hiereus*, is simply not found any-where in Paul's letters nor in any other New Testament writings, with three exceptions: with reference to the Jerusalem priests in the Gospels, to Jesus' own ultimate and conclusive priesthood in the letter to the Hebrews (e.g., 5:6; 7:1-23), and to the priestly status of God's people *collectively* in Revelation (1:6; 5:10; 20:6). In John of Patmos's perspective, not only was the sacrificial system obsolete, but so was the very concept of temple, being replaced by the premonarchic image of God's dwelling in a tent surrounded by God's people (Rev. 21:3, 22; cf. 2 Sam. 7:1-7). Being "priests," therefore, meant not a formal religious office but an implication and responsibility of one's baptism, that is, to offer one's very life in praise of and service to God.

How did this wide variety of nonpriestly ministries evolve into the three-part ministry of *diakonoi* (servants), *presbyteroi* (elders), and *episkopoi* (overseers) understood by the latest New Testament writers? While we will never know the precise details of this process, we can see one portrayal of the rough outlines in the story Luke tells in Acts.

After the first Easter, Luke portrays the Jerusalem disciples gathered around the leadership of "the Twelve," a group also referred to in the Gospels (e.g., Matt. 10:1-4; Mark 3:14-19; John 6:67-71). One should note that although much later theology envisions the Twelve in lofty social terms (e.g., saints, first priests, bishops, or pope), their actual status was as lowly rural fishermen and other "nobodies." Although Luke's audience may have been the urban elite, he, like the other Gospel writers, portrays the first people who ministered in the name of Jesus as persons without the slightest official credentials. The Holy Spirit speaks to the rich and powerful through the voice of the poor and marginalized.

Their first ministerial act is an elaborate ritual in which Matthias is selected to replace Judas Iscariot among this group (Acts 1:16-26). However, Luke rarely again refers to this group, showing instead the actions of individual representatives of the *ekklēsia* or of the *ekklēsia* as a collective entity. There is a certain tongue-in-cheek irony to Luke's narrative on the theme of ministry: humans propose, but the Holy Spirit disposes. For instance, when it emerges that the Greek-speaking widows are being neglected in the daily distribution of bread, the Twelve announce as one:

> It is not right that we should neglect the word of God in order to serve at tables. Therefore, brothers, select from among yourselves seven men of good standing, full of the Spirit and of wisdom, whom we may appoint to this task, while we, for our part, will devote ourselves to prayer and to serving the word. (Acts 6:2-4)

They appoint seven good men for this task, who are never portrayed as "serving at tables," but only in the act of proclaiming the Word! This comic portrayal is part of Luke's ongoing narrative reflecting the way in which the *ekklēsia* constantly must subject its own ideas to the plan of the Holy Spirit.

As the narrative continues and the *ekklēsia* grows and spreads, Luke shows it dealing with various issues for the first time, including the way in which Gentiles are to be admitted into church membership; the relationship between external, official authority and the behavior of the *ekklēsia;* and the "translation" of the Good News into forms that can be heard by people of diverse cultural backgrounds. During this process of trial and error, ministry slowly begins to separate into three overlapping ranges of function. First, there was the kind of practical service provided to widows and others in need: the giving of daily bread and other basic necessities of life. Given the intent fully to integrate economics into the life of the *ekklēsia*, making sure that people are fed, housed, and clothed was seen as a central ministerial function. Second, there was the need to clarify authentic discipleship teachings and practices from false or incomplete ones. Throughout Acts, we find various situations in which such ministry is provided (e.g., 18:24-26; 19:1-5). Finally, as the *ekklēsia* begins to develop a tradition that is to be passed on across generations, there developed a need for leadership that ensured both continuity and pastoral care. Out of these basic needs and in light of the inherited traditions of Hebrew Scriptures, the *ekklēsia* began to develop a sense of the wisdom of elders (e.g., Acts 15) and the authority of overseers (Acts 20:28). As always, these diverse forms of ministry were to operate for the common good and the building up of the *ekklēsia*.

Although Acts offers a few hints at how ministry in the *ekklēsia* evolved into categories appropriated and transformed by later generations into a fixed structure, it does not present this three-part ministry as separate from or above the other forms of ministry of which Paul speaks in First Corinthians, as shown earlier in this section. For instance, although in light of later developments we have traced the role of elders and overseers back to Acts (and, of course, back to the Hebrew Scriptures and Greco-Roman practices), if one were simply to read Acts looking for what Luke seems to consider the most important ministries, one might see missionary evangelizing and pastoral care to the *ekklēsia* as foremost, at least in terms of narrative frequency. From Acts 1:8 on, Luke prepares readers to see the primary ministerial role to be as Jesus' witnesses throughout the world via the power of the Holy Spirit. We will look more at this particular function in chapter 5. It seems worth noting this now, though, in order to underscore the fact that focusing ministry around "deacon, elder, and overseer" was a later development, not an original aspect of the *ekklēsia*'s self-understanding.

Similarly, the notion that people are ordained in what some theologians might call an ontologically transformative event (i.e., the very being of the person ordained is changed by the ordination rite) is nowhere found nor hinted at in the New Testament. A look at a ritual that is portrayed in Acts and often associated with ordination, the laying on of hands, shows how the purpose of the ritual is not setting persons aside for a particular, lifelong ministry, but providing one way among others in which the Holy Spirit is given to people for various purposes. Consider the five occasions when Luke tells of the laying on of hands:

- The appointing of the Seven to the ministry of service to the widows (6:3-6)

- In confirmation of the baptism of people in Samaria (8:14-17)

- Ananias's healing touch upon Saul (9:17)

- Prophets and teachers in the *ekklēsia* in Antioch setting Barnabas and Saul apart for the work of preaching to the Gentiles (13:1-4)

- Paul confirming the baptism into Jesus of twelve disciples of John the Baptist in Ephesus (19:1-7)

There is no factor unifying either those who lay on hands or those upon whom hands are laid, nor the purpose for the act, other than disciples supporting and strengthening other disciples to receive the Holy Spirit's help on the journey in the Way. It is not until the much later text of 1 Timothy 4:14 that one hears of laying on of hands in a more formal sense by the council of elders (Greek *presbytērion*). But even there, it refers back to the "gift" given to Timothy, who is elsewhere in the New Testament repeatedly referred to simply as Paul's "co-worker" and "brother," and not as holder of any formal ministerial office (e.g., Acts 16:1-3; Rom. 16:21; 1 Cor. 4:17; 16:10; Phil. 1:1).

Apart from the laying on of hands, there is no other ritual named or described in the New Testament's earlier texts that suggests that persons called by the Holy Spirit to engage in a particular ministerial activity are transformed in any way other than in receiving the Spirit, a gift given to each and every member of the *ekklēsia* for the common good.

Given the total integration of economics into the life of the *ekklēsia*, the more modern sense of a separation between "ecclesial" ministries (i.e., "church" work) and "secular" ministries (i.e., a sense that one's ordinary, everyday domestic and vocational acts are a form of ministry when done as service to God and God's people) makes no sense when considering the early *ekklēsia*. As we will see in the following two chapters, both the internal and the external life of discipleship involve the joyous task of proclaiming and living out the Good News of Jesus. That such activity should come to be seen as burdensome or resembling the daily grind of going to work for many in our society could in no way be foreseen by the early *ekklēsia*. As Jesus says in John's Gospel, "My food is to do the will of the One who sent me and to complete that work" (John 4:34). For Jesus, doing God's will was *nourishing*, not draining. Certainly such an attitude accompanied both Paul and others sent out by the Holy Spirit to continue that work. Despite the physical hardships and experience of frequent rejection, Paul constantly expresses the joy he feels in performing his ministry and that he finds amongst church members around the Mediterranean (e.g., Rom. 15:32; 2 Cor. 2:3-4; 2 Cor. 8:1-3; Phil. 1:4; 1 Thess. 1:6). Perhaps if we find many in ministry today suffering from depression or "burnout" it is because the church today has often come more to resemble an organization engaged in the fierce competition of marketing programs rather than a celebratory assembly of sisters and brothers rejoicing together in the diverse gifts of the Holy Spirit.

Reflection Questions

1. What tasks or roles do you associate with the terms "ministry" and "minister"? Do you consider the daily work of all the baptized to be "ministry"? Why or why not? What would be different if people were "ordained" to such ministries as carpentry, food growing or preparation, or child care?

2. Consider how persons are called to ministry in your faith community. What is the relationship between individual and communal discernment in this process? How does this compare to the picture of the early church presented in this chapter?

3. Consider the lives of people you know or see who are in church ministry, whether clergy or lay. Is their work nourishing "food" as it was for Jesus or do they come across as overly busy or burdened? How does their relationship with the other members of the congregation reinforce or challenge this situation?

5

The Mission in the World

A basic notion that both followers of Jesus and supporters of the Roman order had in common was that all of creation was subject to ultimate, divine authority. The God who called Jesus to preach the Good News of God's reign had long been proclaimed as the Creator of all that is. Similarly, Roman religion, along with the various indigenous traditions of the Mediterranean, envisioned a network of divine beings with power over all, from the empire itself to local streams and glades. The two traditions—although defenders of each often expressed deep suspicion and even contempt for the other—shared an understanding that the realm of religion included not just that of prayer and ritual performed periodically in temples or in the streets on particular days but all of life, all the time.

This is another area where our modern Western separation of religion and society leaves us unprepared to comprehend the constant proclamation and practice of divine power in the streets and marketplaces of New Testament cities. In our world, those who would invoke God or the Bible on urban street corners are generally seen as "nuts," independent of what one might think of the specific message they may be offering. Even more on the margins are those who would dare to take seriously the biblical disciplines of healing and exorcising those suffering from various diseases and disabilities. But there is no doubt that each of these three practices—preaching the gospel, healing the sick, and exorcising unclean and demonic spirits—was commanded by Jesus to his disciples and carried out in the *ekklēsia* (e.g., Mark 6:7-13; Matt. 10:5-9; Luke 9:1-6; Acts 3:1-8; 4:2; 5:42; 16:18; 19:11-12). Are acts of healing and exorcism obsolete today in light of our "superior" knowledge of medicine and psychiatry? Or might the early *ekklēsia* have understood something about the maintenance of physical, mental, and spiritual wholeness that we have forgotten and would do well to recover? If Christians continue to see themselves as bearers of Good News, why is the church so frequently hesitant to speak publicly of putting trust in God in all things? As we have been doing throughout this book, we will begin our consideration of these questions by looking briefly at how such practices were viewed in ancient Israel and in the cities of the Greco-Roman world of Jesus' time.

Proclaiming the Word of YHWH in Israel

We have seen in earlier chapters how Israel's prophets saw their task as calling the people to a renewed commitment to the covenant through the powerful proclamation of God's Word. This function took place in a wide variety of circumstances and contexts: direct one-on-one confrontation with the kings of Israel and Judah (e.g., 2 Sam. 7, 12; 1 Kgs. 22:8-28); oracular denunciations of the idolatry and selfishness of the wealthy elite likely delivered from a distance (e.g., Amos 4; Mic. 6; Isa. 58; Ezek. 16); or literary critiques of such behavior preserved in writing by the prophet's followers (e.g., Jer. 36). What all these diverse forms of preaching have in common is that they were all divinely inspired speech directed exclusively to God's covenanted people. Although many passages speak of the prophet's being directed to "prophesy against the nations," it is almost certain that only Israelites were hearers or readers of such texts. In casting divine judgment on the nations, the prophets were not aiming to "convert" Gentiles but to remind God's people that their God was God of *all* the nations, even if those other nations did not know of or trust in the name of YHWH.

It is this assumption that makes for the humorous twist in the book of Jonah. The word of YHWH tells Jonah to "Go at once to Nineveh, that great city, and cry out against it; for their wickedness has come up before me" (Jonah 1:2). But rather than heed the divine command, Jonah flees in the opposite direction, setting up the famous encounter between Jonah and the great fish. Eventually Jonah can run no more and begins the arduous task of walking the three days' journey across the great city, crying out, "Forty days more, and Nineveh shall be overthrown!" Nineveh, the capital of the Assyrian empire which conquered the northern kingdom of Israel in 722 B.C.E., was long despised by Israel as a foreign oppressor. That such an arrogant people should even consider responding to the lonely voice of Jonah seems about as likely as such an event occurring in today's New York City. Yet in the very next verse, the narrator tells us, "And the people of Nineveh believed God; they proclaimed a fast, and everyone, great and small, put on sackcloth" (Jonah 3:4-5). But rather than rejoice in this spectacular event, which leads to God's change of heart over the fate of Nineveh, Jonah angrily sulks. God works with the temperamental prophet to teach him that God's mercy is at least as important as God's judgment. The point of the short book is not to relate a historical report about the instant conversion of the Assyrians. Rather, it is to remind *Israel* of the abundance of God's loving mercy that yearns for the return of the heart of God's own people back to the covenant with which their relationship had begun. It works as a story with a twist precisely because the idea that a prophet would actually be sent out to seek the conversion of Gentiles is so unprecedented as to seem absurd to the writer's audience.

Israel's tradition of prophetic preaching, then, was solely for the purpose of reminding the people of their own relationship with YHWH. In this way, it resembles what most Christians experience today in the Sunday sermon or in occasional documents from church leaders to the people. Outsiders would certainly be welcome to listen to or read such proclamations, but only with the understanding that they are overhearing an "in-house" conversation.

Prophets were not the only ones who brought God's Word to the people. Frequently we hear simply of a "messenger" (Hebrew *mal'akh*; Greek *angelos*) who informs people of news that turns out to be of divine origin. It is often unclear from the narrative context whether such messengers are to be understood simply as humans or as "angels." In both biblical languages, this ambiguity is usually left unresolved, precisely to make the point that God's messengers are not always easy to identify (e.g., Gen. 18; Tob. 5:4-5; cf. Heb. 13:2). English translators must collapse these narrative tensions by choosing between "messenger" and "angel." But in either case, we see the tradition of divine proclamation being announced only to members of the nation of Israel.

But Israel's understanding that YHWH was the God of all people did come to have an effect on the direction and content of the preaching tradition in later centuries. For example, the speeches of Micah and the postexilic author of Isaiah 56-66 speak to Israel of a time in which the Gentiles will come to Jerusalem to share in the worship of YHWH (e.g., Mic. 4:1-4; Isa. 60; 64). As with the story of Jonah, though, these prophecies were meant to initiate not the process of ingathering of the nations but of reassuring Israel in difficult times that YHWH remained fully in charge of all history.

Throughout the period between the end of the prophetic writings of the Hebrew Scriptures and that of Jesus, this pattern of speaking *of* the nations but only *to* God's people continued. As scholars have shown, there is virtually no evidence of Jews in the Mediterranean cities attempting to preach about YHWH to their Gentile neighbors. So entrenched was this tradition of insularity that the first-century C.E. Roman historian Tacitus describes the Jews with the ignorance and contempt born of the absence of intercultural dialogue:

[The Jews] regard the rest of humanity with all the hatred of enemies. They sit apart at meals, they sleep apart, and though, as a nation, they are singularly prone to lust, they abstain from intercourse with foreign women. . . .(Tacitus, *Histories,* book 5)

To understand just what it was that Tacitus saw as so disgusting about the Jews, we must look at Greco-Roman attitudes toward and practices of "preaching."

Preaching Good News in Greek and Roman Traditions

While Israel's faith insisted that all of history and creation were under YHWH's constant attention, Greek thinking developed what we might refer to as "secular" wisdom alongside the diversity of religious traditions found throughout the Mediterranean. As far back as archaeological and written evidence go, we find peoples in this region engaged in religious rituals of thanksgiving, propitiation, and petitioning of divine spirits. But along the way, traditions developed that came to define the Greek worldview in terms of *philosophy.* Schools of thought promulgated by such figures as Plato, Aristotle, and Zeno competed for centuries to establish rational principles that explained the structures of life and the human role within both nature and society. Such powerful thinkers continue, of course, to be taught and discussed to this day. Proponents of these various schools of thought frequently attempted to engage in public debate and argument, each proffering their own views as superior. In places such as Athens, such public proclamations of philosophical wisdom were not only tolerated; they were sought out as popular entertainment, not unlike the earlier American tradition of mounting one's soapbox to deliver one's opinions (e.g., Acts 17:17-33).

A key question for Jews then, as for Christians throughout the centuries, was, How much do these philosophical traditions "compete" with divinely revealed concepts and commandments and how much do they provide helpful tools for deeper understanding of the biblical traditions? Then as now, there are no easy answers to this question. In a center of literacy and learning such as Alexandria, Jewish writers such as Philo attempted to "translate" biblical narratives into philosophical language that could be understood and accepted by Hellenistic Gentiles. Jews in other places, however, sometimes saw such efforts as misguided, interpreting such projects as part of a larger effort to accommodate Jewish traditions to outsiders' cultures (see, e.g., 1 Macc. 1:11-15). One might note similar struggles over the use of Platonic thought by Augustine, Aristotelian thought by Thomas Aquinas, and more recently, Marxian economics by liberation theologians. The line between "secular philosophy" and "idolatry" has not always been easy for some to draw.

A sharper line could, though, be drawn when the question was more explicitly that of Greco-Roman religions. One of the aspects of Judaism that was viewed as so abhorrent by Romans such as Tacitus was its insistent *monotheism*. In a world where differences in cultural and religious traditions were often accepted simply as a matter of "same gods, different names," most Jews stubbornly refused to see Jupiter or Zeus as merely another name for YHWH. Furthermore, the very multiplicity of gods and goddesses recognized by virtually all other peoples in the region was contrary to the heart of the Torah commandment to "have no other gods" before YHWH (e.g., Exod. 20:3; cf. Deut. 6:4-5). From the Roman perspective, such exclusivism was seen as arrogant and antisocial. From the Jewish perspective, of course, it was part of the eternal struggle to worship "YHWH alone" while living amidst other peoples and their religions.

Aside from the unique Jewish rejection of Greco-Roman forms of worship, other cultures usually found it easy to accept their neighbors' religious traditions. This was especially true in the time of the Roman empire, when wars, famine, and economic dislocation had forced many people to flee their homelands for life in the urban centers of trade and commerce. What had been locally "dominant" cultures were now frequently experienced as part of a larger mix of customs, not unlike Asian, African, and Latin American immigrants and refugees adapting to life in New York or Los Angeles. While one might have felt more comfortable staying with "one's own" in an urban neighborhood—as have numerous first-generation immigrants to the United States—there was tremendous economic opportunity awaiting those who reached out to people beyond their familiar group. For those of polytheistic outlook, such a move was seen not as a "sellout" but as a natural adaptation to changed circumstances.

The result of this situation was that little effort was made to "evangelize" one's neighbors. Many religions were available in cities such as Corinth or Ephesus, brought in from places such as Phrygia, Greece, or Egypt. While some people's decision to join a particular religious group might have been made on the basis of seeking answers to life's questions, most people probably chose to join for more practical reasons. For example, given the lack of a civic or other institutional "safety net," becoming part of a religion provided a form of social security for those engaged in a trade. In addition, people attending rituals at shrines and temples would find great opportunity for making business contacts among their fellow worshipers. In other words, as in the United States today, individuals often found religious affiliation *useful* for one reason or another, without feeling a need or desire to persuade others to join them in their specific choice.

The central exception to this situation was the growing hegemony of the imperial cult. Rome, like most empires, saw the practice of traditional religion as helpful to its goal of social control. A given people which recognized some form of traditional religious leadership could be manipulated through imperial control of that leadership. For the Jews, this meant garnering imperial loyalty among the Jerusalem elite (e.g., Ezra 7:26; John 19:15). Such agreements were, of course, enriching for the elite and impoverishing for the masses. But so long as the religious leadership maintained social stability and assured the flow of taxes, there was little short of violent revolution that ordinary people could do to affect the arrangements. The development of the practice of worshiping the Roman royal family itself, though, took this arrangement a large step further. Other polytheistic nations might have previously looked upon the Jewish people as simply strange for their monotheism. With the advent of the imperial cult, Jewish practice bordered on the *illegal*. It was only an official exemption from the requirement of participation in emperor worship that saved the Jews from an ancient holocaust. Nonetheless, the imperial cult became a ubiquitous feature of city life beginning in the middle of the first century of the common era. In statues, plaques, inscriptions, and parades, one could not avoid the proclamation that the emperor was divine. It was into this world that Paul and others came, proclaiming throughout the land the "Good News" of Jesus, the Risen One.

Proclaiming the Gospel of God's Reign

The Gospel texts make clear that Jesus himself did not go outside the Palestinian region with his message and only rarely spoke it to non-Jews. Certainly this was Matthew's understanding, as he quotes Jesus saying, "I was sent only to the lost sheep of the house of Israel" (Matt. 15:24; cf. Mark 7:27). Matthew's Jesus expressly confines the command to the Twelve to preach the Good News to these same lost sheep, telling them to "go nowhere among the Gentiles and enter no town of the Samaritans" (Matt. 10:5-7). Luke, likely writing for a Gentile audience, omits this restriction from his parallel passage (Luke 9:2).

At the very end of Matthew's Gospel, however, we hear the risen Jesus make a seemingly contradictory statement: "Go therefore and make disciples of all nations" (Matt. 28:19). Matthew thus appears to understand the Easter event as initiating a new age not conceivable even by Jesus during his lifetime. With the resurrection, not only is "God's people" open to the Gentiles, but disciples are explicitly to become *missionaries* to the Gentiles.

While Matthew ends without narrating such a mission, Luke wrote the book of Acts precisely to portray the trials and tribulations of those sent out on mission, starting from Jerusalem "to the ends of the earth" (Acts 1:8). His schematic and highly stylized account is joined in the New Testament by the collection of letters written in Paul's name to provide an unprecedented picture of Jews preaching a religious message to Gentiles. That such a program was opposed by the Jewish synagogue communities goes without saying. But it was even controversial among Jewish followers of Jesus, who were not at all clear that Jesus' ministry and resurrection meant undertaking such a mission. After all, there were numerous, seemingly intractable problems that such a course created. For instance, what would the idea that Jesus was "the Christ" (Messiah/Anointed One) mean to those not steeped in Hebrew Scriptures? How would the long-hated doctrine of monotheism play among the nations? How could people accept that someone crucified as a criminal by the Romans in an obscure outpost of empire was truly the agent of the Creator of all? These and other theological and cultural barriers must have seemed insurmountable to many. Further, what happened if Gentiles actually accepted the message? Would they thereby become "Jews" or something altogether new? Did adult males need to be circumcised? Were the provisions of the Torah now applicable to Gentiles claiming trust in Jesus?

While we cannot engage each of these and other related questions here, perhaps it suffices to raise them to point out how complex, both in theory and in practice, a mission to the Gentiles must have seemed to the early *ekklēsia*. But apart from these difficulties, an even more central one loomed. In referring to the message of Jesus' as "gospel" or "Good News" (Greek *euangelion*), the *ekklēsia* was aiming a dagger at the heart of imperial propaganda. While *euangelion* is found over seventy times in the New Testament, it is used only once in all of the Septuagint (2 Sam. 4:10). The clear reason for this is that the term was not one brought forward from Israel's tradition, but one *expropriated from the Roman empire*. "Good news" to imperial residents meant either the birth of a new emperor or the proclamation of an edict from an established emperor. For Mark's Gospel to open with "the beginning of the good news of Jesus Christ" was to challenge the emperor's claim to divinely established authority right from the start of Mark's story. Similarly, the New Testament's use of the related verb *euangelizō*, "to announce" or "to preach," was to engage in the active process of proclaiming Jesus, not Caesar, worthy of "faith" (Greek *pistis*, a similarly appropriated imperial term from the Latin *fides*) and worship. With the verb form, there was some overlap with Septuagint usage. The word is used twenty-four times, almost always in the context of the question of royal authority, human or divine (human authority: e.g., 1 Sam. 31:9; 2 Sam. 18:19-31; 1 Kgs. 1:42; divine authority: e.g., Ps. 40:9; 95:2; Isa. 40:9; 52:7; 60:6). Thus, New Testament phrases such as "to proclaim the eternal good news" (Rev. 14:6; Greek *euangelion aiōnion euangelisai*) apply the tradition of YHWH's exclusive rule over the nations to the joining of the risen Jesus in that reign, as proclaimed by the *ekklēsiai*.

But most frequently used as the verb of "preaching" in the New Testament is the Greek *kēryssō*. The secular Greek meaning of the term almost always involves *public* proclamation of an important message. Similarly, its use in the Septuagint, while not always involving a religious message, is invariably public (e.g., Prov. 1:21; Dan. 3:4). Whether with or without *euangelion*, the New Testament consistently uses this term to refer to the public preaching of God's Word. First among Jews in Judea and Galilee, and then out to Gentiles throughout the Roman empire, the *ekklēsia* clearly understood itself to be called to proclaim a joyous but subversive message to all who would listen.

As Acts and Paul's letters frequently show, the "reward" for such preaching could include ridicule, arrest, assault, or even death. Whether at the hands of fellow Jews, who saw followers of Jesus as heretics, or Roman citizens, who saw them as treasonous, members of the *ekklēsia* sent out to preach were taking great risks (e.g., John 15:18-20; 16:1-2). But the other side of the coin was the joyous work of offering the truth of God's Word and way of life to people caught up in the lies, exploitation, and cycle of violence endemic to empire. Like farmers casting seeds, there would be no greater satisfaction for the *ekklēsia* than to see those seeds sprout, grow and bear a rich harvest (e.g., Mark 4).

Healing the Sick and Expelling Unclean Spirits

One of the most remarkable aspects of the Gospels' stories about Jesus and his ministry is the frequency with which Jesus is found in the presence of people suffering from a variety of physical, mental, and spiritual ailments. The fact of such suffering was not in itself remarkable, of course. In the ancient world, as in many parts of ours today, the ravages of disease, accidental injury accompanied by untreated infections, infant and maternal mortality, and the like were commonplace. What is unusual is how much narrative energy is focused on the plight of such people in comparison with earlier biblical tradition.

Healing in the Hebrew Scriptures

Consider the contrasting situation portrayed in Genesis. Despite the harsh conditions of desert migration and periodic famine, not a single person is reported to be sick or to die prematurely because of illness. Rachel's death during her second childbirth only proves the rule by its exceptional nature: that so many children could be born without a single infant or childhood death is such an extraordinarily unlikely feat that it can only be explained as a consequence of God's repeated promise to Abraham, Sarah, and their descendants that God's blessing would make them as numerous as the stars of the sky or the sand of the seashore.

Exodus and other texts explicating the legal provisions of the Torah consider ill health in theory but not as a narrative fact, again with but a few exceptions. Numerous provisions are made for isolation and priestly observation of persons suffering from various ailments, including such normal occurrences as menstrual bleeding. The book of Numbers reports massive deaths as a result of rebellion against the authority of Moses (and hence, of

YHWH), attributed to divine fire, a swallowing up by the earth, and a "plague" (Num. 16; cf. 25:1-9). Some scholars have interpreted this account as an after-the-fact theological explanation for an epidemic of disease. While this may be so, the fact that the narrative tells it in terms of rebellion and punishment underscores the apparent reticence of the Hebrew Scriptures to deal directly with the ubiquity of natural illness.

Throughout the Hebrew Scriptures this pattern continues. Illness is regularly seen as the consequence of failure to live the covenant. Thus, the proper response to ill health is not treatment of a person's physical symptoms but a change in the behavior that brought on the illness. For instance, in the sabbatical and jubilee provisions in Leviticus, we find the promise of life experienced as bountiful and harmonious when lived in accordance with Torah balanced by its opposite if the people refuse to practice jubilee. God will "bring terror on you; consumption and fever that waste the eyes and cause life to pine away" (Lev. 26:16). The remedy for this fever is not to concoct an herbal medicine or offer a ritual spell as in many tribal traditions, but for *the entire society* to become obedient to YHWH through the practice of economic and social justice (cf. Deut. 28:15-68; 32:15-25).

Certainly much of this tradition resulted from the wrenching experience of the destruction of Jerusalem and exile to Babylon, an event "predicted" by the Deuteronomic texts mentioned above. The prophets Jeremiah and Ezekiel, in speaking directly of the horror of this cataclysmic event, speak in language very similar to that of Deuteronomy (e.g., Jer. 14:12; 21:3-9; Ezek. 5:5-17). Hence, the postexilic reestablishment of Jerusalem and its priestly regime emphasized over and over that Israel's collective health was a direct result of its fidelity to YHWH's rules of order (e.g., Neh. 1:5-9; 1 Chr. 6:24-27).

At the same time, there was clearly an awareness of various ailments that seemed to befall certain people apart from their loyalty to Torah. Leviticus contains a long set of procedures for dealing with skin diseases and similar situations (e.g., Lev. 13:42-46). In the absence of a modern understanding of microbial contagion, this system, grounded in many generations' experiences of sudden, catastrophic epidemics, responded to the presence of such conditions with an eye toward the health of the wider community. The presence of this kind of condition generated a vicious logic: the illness necessitated putting the person outside the camp, where one was denied not only any possible physical help one might need but also the psychological and spiritual support that contribute to healing and wholeness.

Thus, we see a dual response to sickness in the Hebrew Scriptures. Some physical conditions are clearly the result of social injustice and call for treatment not so much of the specific symptom as of a broader awareness among all community members of the connection between their bodily health and their degree of covenant fidelity. At the same time, there are other conditions that were understood to be irruptions of chaos into the social order and hence could be remedied by separating "clean" from "unclean" according to God's original design (Gen. 1).

A rare biblical focus on individual ill health is found in the cycle of healings attributed to the prophets Elijah and Elisha (1 Kgs. 17; 2 Kgs. 4:32-37; 5). The healings come in the midst of the narrative of Israel's corrupt and idolatrous kings. Within this context, they suggest that although YHWH is not supportive of the royal establishment, it does not mean that YHWH's power is not present among the people. The gift of healing shared by both prophets is part of their larger grant of spiritual authority to speak truth to power in the name of God. The Gospel writers, beginning with Mark, surely have these stories in mind as they portray Jesus' own healing power centuries later.

In an even more extreme contrast with the Gospels, the Hebrew Scriptures virtually never speak of a phenomenon central to Jesus' ministry and that of his followers: persons possessed by unclean or evil spirits. The only person ever described in such a condition is the disgraced king Saul, who, shockingly to modern ears, is said to be possessed of "an evil spirit from YHWH" (1 Sam. 16:14-23; 18:10; 19:9). There is no question of attempting to remedy Saul's condition, for it is said to have resulted directly from "the spirit of YHWH depart[ing]" after Saul has failed to keep YHWH's command (1 Sam. 16:14). Only a single reference, in the book of Zechariah, speaks of an "unclean spirit," but it is one occupying the land as a whole, not an individual person (Zech. 13:2). God will remove this spirit, says the prophet, as part of the process of preparing Jerusalem to be rebuilt after the exile.

Healing in Greco-Roman Society

Greco-Roman society was filled with stories and rituals dealing with issues of health and wholeness. From the ongoing image of Hippocrates as "the father of medicine," to numerous healing shrines such as the shrine to Asclepius, Hellenistic culture applied great resources to the problem. For the overwhelming majority of urban residents in the first century, though, such sophisticated means of healing were far removed from their daily lives. Instead, most people turned to local folk and family traditions of healing, whether through homeopathic remedies or shamanistic rituals. As we find increasingly the case today in the United States, formally trained healthcare practitioners were available for the wealthy, but ordinary folks and the poor tended to turn to whatever might work.

In attempting to cure the wide variety of ailments with which people might be afflicted, ancient healers considered every possible means of causation. Perhaps primary among the causes of illness was what anthropologists refer to as "spirit aggression." That is, the symptoms observed in a person's body or behavior were attributed to disturbances in the person's system caused by the presence of invading spirits of one kind or another. These spirits were not necessarily understood as "evil" in the sense of the tradition of exorcism, nor could their effects be limited to what we would consider today to be "mental illness" or epilepsy. Virtually any ailment might have as its cause the presence of a spiritual entity disrupting a person's being. Given the eventual discovery of the wide variety of invisible-to-the-eye, disease-causing agents, ancient healers were not unreasonable in understanding illness in this way.

People may have become healers in the Greco-Roman world for a variety of reasons, many familiar to us: increased social honor and prestige, personal profit, or the good of the community. In a village or tribal context, a healer would likely have been the local holy person, whose shamanic powers enabled him or her to tap into divine energy for the good of a community member. In an urban, multicultural context, however, such a basic sense of the common good would likely have been replaced by more personal motives. This distinction is crucial to understanding the difference between Jesus' actions as healer and exorcist in rural Galilee and those of his followers in the urban *ekklēsia*.

Healing in the Ekklēsia

In the Gospels, Jesus' acts of healing and casting out unclean or evil spirits are regularly shown being confronted by the defenders of the status quo. They do not challenge his possession of healing power, but instead claim that his use of it is illegal, blasphemous, and even a manifestation of Beelzebul (e.g., Mark 2:3-12; 3:1-6, 22). Throughout these stories, both Jesus and the Gospel narrators make clear that what Jesus is doing is not only about restoring the body's physical health but also about restoring the excluded individual to wholeness of membership in the community, and hence, of mind and spirit. Our atomized conception of the human person and his or her relationship to society might conceive of these as independent actions on different components of the individual. However, Jesus' more holistic anthropology understood the healing of body and social status to be part of a single cause-and-effect relationship. Thus, the language used to describe the effects of Jesus' actions include not only ordinary Greek words for healing, but the more inclusive *sōzō:* "to heal" but also "to save" (e.g., Mark 5:34; 10:52). To remove one's physical ailment *is* to return a person to full dignity and status, a teaching made poignantly clear in the doubled stories of two women of initially opposite social locations, each of whom becomes "daughter" through Jesus' healing act (Mark 5:21-43).

Jesus' challenge to the healing practices of his time included a frontal assault on the "conventional wisdom's" link between illness or disability and sinfulness. This is shown most graphically in the story of the person born blind in John 9. Jesus' own disciples mouth the dominant perspective in asking whose sin it was that caused someone's lifelong inability to see. The tradition linking parental sin with the child's ailment had already been challenged by Jeremiah centuries earlier (Jer. 31:27-31, implicitly challenging Exod. 34:7). However, it continued to hold sway among many, perhaps because of the scribal elite's need to explain away the massive suffering of the poor as somehow the poor's own fault and hence not a result of the elite's greed and injustice. Jesus reverses the terms of discussion from "blindness = sin" to "seeing without responding = sin." The Jerusalem authorities and their supporters can only perceive through the eyes they've been given by a system that has resulted in tremendous inequality of wealth, status, and dignity. In calling the blind one to "wash in the pool which means Sent," Jesus not only breaks the link between blindness and sin; he forges a new one between *sight* and *discipleship*. The one who has learned to see is cast out of his old, dark, imprisoning social order in order to be "born again" into a discipleship community whose path is illuminated by the One who is the Light of the World.

It is this call that leads the early *ekklēsia* to continue Jesus' own ministry of healing and exorcising. In Acts 3:1-8 and 14:8-18, Peter and Paul respectively follow in the footsteps walked by Jesus in Luke 5:17-26. In the first incident, Peter and John encounter at the Jerusalem Temple gate a person unable to walk since birth. Refusing his expected receipt of alms, Peter gazes intently at the man's eyes and says:

> "I have no silver or gold, but what I have I give you; in the name of Jesus Christ of Nazareth, stand up and walk."
> And he took him by the right hand and raised him up;

and immediately his feet and ankles were made strong. Jumping up, he stood and began to walk, and he entered the temple with them, walking and leaping and praising God. (Acts 3:6-8)

Peter's act of healing is explicitly performed in the name of Jesus, not for the sake of Peter's own enrichment or increased honor. Indeed, before the event is complete, Peter and John are arrested by the angry Temple elite (4:1-3). The newly empowered beggar responds not only with prayerful, enthusiastic joy but also by "clinging" to Peter and John (3:11). As with the blind beggar in John's Gospel, his experience of healing is both physical and social, leading him to form new bonds with members of the discipleship community.

Just as Jesus' acts of healing were continued by his disciples, so were his exorcisms. In fact, Acts tells of all three of Jesus' commands under discussion in this chapter taking place as an integrated pattern of discipleship activity:

Philip went down to the city of Samaria and proclaimed the Messiah to them. The crowds with one accord listened eagerly to what was said by Philip, hearing and seeing the signs that he did, for unclean spirits, crying with loud shrieks, came out of many who were possessed; and many others who were paralyzed or lame were cured. So there was great joy in that city. (Acts 8:5-6; cf. 5:15-16)

Preaching, healing, and exorcising are thus portrayed not as independent ministries but as a program for generating social and physical *jubilee*: a "starting over" in the whole person that enables people to experience life as joyful rather than as oppressive. These three activities together offered an integrated approach to healing and wholeness. A person who heard the gospel but whose spirit was still possessed by an unclean spirit would not be able to respond freely to the preached Word (e.g., Mark 4:15). Similarly, one whose body had been healed but who had not heard the Word would not know the meaning for their life of having been healed by the power of the one true God (e.g., Acts 14:8-18). Preaching and healing had different cultural understandings in biblical and in Greco-Roman traditions, but the *ekklēsia* understood its own call to transcend either of these specific healing traditions in favor of the preaching and practice of Jesus.

For we who are indoctrinated into Western notions of medicine and psychology, the practice of healing and exorcism may be the most difficult discipleship activities to consider incorporating into church life today. Many people tend either to slough off these New Testament stories as part of a "primitive" mind-set or to attribute them to the unique holiness or powers of people like Peter or Paul. Recent studies of indigenous healing and exorcism traditions suggest, however, that we may stand to benefit from reconsidering the applicability of Jesus' commands to heal and exorcise to our situation.

For instance, cross-cultural studies have noted the remarkable similarity between the New Testament accounts and Native American, African, and Asian traditions of spirit-healing. For peoples whose anthropologies see a continuity rather than a split between the physical and social/spiritual aspects of human life, any healing process must necessarily include actions aimed at the person as they are embedded in their specific social situation. This is not a matter of "magic" in the sense of verbal formulae that allegedly can produce results, but of prayerful communion between the healer and the one to be healed. We see this in the account from Acts discussed above, where Peter "gazed intently" at the disabled beggar before speaking with and touching him. Similarly, recall the Gospel story in which Jesus' disciples fail to exorcise an unclean spirit from a possessed child because they apparently were relying on their own power rather than allowing God's Spirit to work through them in prayer (Mark 9:14-29). Once again, we see in Acts a group of itinerant exorcists who attempt to reduce the process to magic only to be humorously (and violently!) rebuffed by the evil spirit who exposes their powerlessness (Acts 19:13-19).

Even our high-tech medical establishment is beginning slowly to recognize this link in its acknowledgment of scientific studies that report the healing power of prayer. For too long Western society has been enthralled by the mechanistic view of the human person that reduces the individual to a biochemical production plant whose parts can be "fixed" as one might a defective carburetor. But the *ekklēsia* understood that at the core of each person was a personality, in Greek *psychē* and Latin *persona*, sometimes translated misleadingly as "soul." The "soul" is not for the biblical person a separable human component but the essence that is greater than, but based on, the sum of the parts. To attempt to heal the *psychē* without addressing bodily and social needs is as futile as is its opposite. We tend to do the former when we offer "spiritual" support that ignores physical needs for food, shelter, and healing (criticized, e.g., in 1 John 3:11-18; Jas. 2:15-16). We tend to do the latter when we offer medical care that knows not how to pray. For Jesus, as for the *ekklēsia,* either route is folly. The joy experienced in Samaria and elsewhere came from their thankful receipt of the *ekklēsia's* offering of healing for the complete person.

Public Witness

One may have noted that in the previous section on preaching, there was no mention of John's Gospel. Indeed, that text never once uses the words for "preaching" or "good news" found so frequently in the Synoptics, Acts, and New Testament letters. Instead, John's Gospel calls on a different semantic field: that of being "sent forth" to "witness."

If preaching the gospel involved announcing the Good News of God's reign, "witness" in the *ekklēsia* involves bringing one's own faith experience into public conversation. In both Hebrew Scripture and the Greco-Roman context, to offer "witness" or "testimony" meant to play a role in a legal process. In contrast to American jurisprudence, a witness in ancient court settings testified not so much to facts and events as to the *reputation* of the person on trial (e.g., Exod. 20:16; 23:1-2). As between YHWH and Israel, each can serve as witness to the reputation of the other: God serves as witness to Israel's faithfulness to the covenant or lack thereof, while Israel can testify that YHWH is indeed God (e.g., Josh. 22:34). When Israel fails to supply this testimony, YHWH can protect his own reputation among the nations (e.g., Ezek. 20:9-22; 36:22). But with rare exceptions, the question of witnessing in the Hebrew Scriptures is an internal question between YHWH and Israel. As with the prophetic vocation to preach, Israel did not see itself called to go out to the Gentiles to speak of God's goodness or holiness. To the extent that other nations discovered YHWH's sovereignty, it was usually in those nations' own experience in relationship to Israel—for example, Egypt's failure to prevent the Exodus or Babylon's inability to keep Jerusalem in ruins and its leaders in exile.

The New Testament extends this function of witnessing into a major category of discipleship activity. The Synoptic Gospels show Jesus preparing disciples for speaking the Good News before Sanhedrins (councils), synagogues, and imperial officials "as a witness to them" (e.g., Mark 13:9-11; Luke 21:12-15). Luke takes up this theme with his many portrayals of the previously cowardly Peter speaking boldly before the Jerusalem Sanhedrin and Paul doing the same before synagogues and Roman governors. But the New Testament text that makes witnessing a central discipleship theme remains John's Gospel. Jesus' predecessor, John, is introduced in the opening verses not as a baptizer but as a witness to the coming of Jesus (John 1:6-9, 15, 19-36). Jesus twice is put on trial by his opponents in Judea, long before what we think of as Holy Week (John 5:17-47; 8:13-59). His witness always serves dual evidentiary purposes: proof of his own status as one sent from God and also that his accusers are the ones who are being judged for their false claim to act in accordance with God's ways. The purpose of this second function is to "shine light in the darkness" so that the "foul deeds" of those who have misled the people can be revealed as grounded not in God's covenant but in a murderous lie (John 3:19-21; 8:37-44).

The importance of this latter goal for the *ekklēsia* can hardly be overemphasized. Both the Jerusalem elite and Roman propaganda proclaimed the status quo as the divine order. But within that status quo, most people lived lives on the edge of survival, while the tiny elite reaped the material and social rewards. One of Jesus' and the *ekklēsia*'s basic projects was to destroy this illusion so that the poor and oppressed could come to see themselves truly as God's beloved children. Just as the process of healing needed to involve the whole person, the task of witness included the positive one of giving testimony to God's love and grace in one's own life as well as the negative one of speaking public truth to power.

The paradigmatic narratives of how this was to work in the *ekklēsia* are told in John 9 and Revelation 11. John's Gospel offers the beautifully constructed account of a blind beggar who gains his sight. Over and over again, those around him ask him to testify to how it happened. As the circles of challenge widen, beginning with neighbors and bystanders, continuing to the Pharisees and finally to the anonymous "them," the newly seeing one develops greater and greater insight into the truth of who Jesus is. At the same time, he discovers the truth about the religious leaders of his time: despite their claims to wisdom and holiness, they are truly blind guides who cannot see God doing a new thing in their midst. Eventually, the blind ones cannot tolerate his insight and expel him from their midst only to have Jesus find him "on the outside" and invite him into the life of discipleship. And the catalyst of this total transformation is simply the healed one's straightforward but insistent testimony: "all I know is, I was blind and now I can see" (John 9:25). This is the model upon which the *ekklēsia* members shape their own witness: all we know is, this is how God has called us from darkness into light, from blindness into sight, from slavery-to-empire into freedom as God's children.

In Revelation 11, this model of individual witness is raised to the level of testimony by the *ekklēsiai* as collective entities. The two witnesses John of Patmos sees in his vision are described as "two lampstands," an image explained earlier in Revelation as representing the *ekklēsiai* themselves (Rev. 11:3-4; 1:20). It is the light from these lamps that will shine in the darkened streets of imperial Ephesus, Smyrna, and so forth. Revelation says that the churches are protected from harm until their witness has been given, but once completed, "the beast that comes up from the abyss will make war on them and conquer them and kill them" (Rev. 11:7). But the beast does not have the final word, for after a short interlude, "a spirit of life from God entered them and they stood on their feet" (11:11). Calling upon the apocalyptic imagery first proclaimed in Daniel 12, Revelation reminds its audience that despite the world's frequent violence against truth tellers, God's resurrection power remains the greater force.

Thus, perhaps paradoxically to us, the New Testament teaches the *ekklēsia* that its public witness will include persecution and violent rejection as well as the joyous awareness of God's presence in the midst of the community as it testifies before the world (e.g., John 15:20; 16:1-2; 17:13-18). For example, after they are flogged by the Jerusalem Sanhedrin for speaking of Jesus, the disciples "rejoiced that they were considered worthy to suffer dishonor for the sake of the name" (Acts 5:27-41). To those silenced by empire's death threats or concern for one's worldly reputation, the idea of offering public witness can seem terrifying. But for those who truly believe that the truth sets people free to live in constant awareness of God's love and abundance, such witness is a joyous opportunity to share the Good News.

If for mainline Christians today healing and exorcising seem strange, the call to public witness often seems an embarrassment embraced only by evangelicals and Jehovah's Witnesses. Living within a secularized culture (despite the high degree of religiosity when compared with other Western nations), believers within liberal churches in the United States have been deeply inculcated into a milieu of "live and let live." The idea of witness seems inextricably linked with "imposing" one's views on others, a notion seemingly abhorrent to the constitutionally protected freedom of religion and right to privacy so cherished within many mainline churches. Most churchgoing Christians in this country have never been present for a public prayer service or religiously motivated demonstration or march nor would they think such activities to be a basic practice of a church which is faithful to the gospel.

And yet the example of faithful witness provided by the early *ekklēsia* requires us to consider this question: Is our reticence a reflection of the gospel or of our desire to fit in comfortably with the surrounding culture? This question has confronted us, of course, at each stage of our reflection on the practice of Jesus' first discipleship communities. What we ask about the motivation underlying our distaste for public witness also applies to the social and economic choices we make in daily life, the forms of liturgy and ministry we model and seek to embody, and so forth. The joy with which the disciples came together for prayer, shared all things in common as sisters and brothers, and spoke boldly to religious and government officials must have been accompanied at times by doubts and fears (e.g., John 14:1, 27; 16:6, 20-22). Jesus didn't expect his followers to stop being human, but to do their best to allow God's Spirit to work through their frail humanity. When they did manage to overcome their fears, Jesus told them, they would be rewarded with true joy and peace, which the world neither knows nor can offer (John 14:27; 15:11; 16:20-25; 33; 17:13). This invitation was both the challenge and the Good News of the call to discipleship within the *ekklēsia*, and remains so to this day.

Reflection Questions

1. What are the most frequent topics of the preaching in your faith community? Does the preaching address the *ekklēsia*'s allegiance to prevailing social and economic conditions? Why or why not? How is such preaching received if and when it is presented? How are conflicts that might arise resolved?

2. Consider your own perspective on the relationship between physical healing, one's societal situation, and prayer. Are these

three completely separate areas for you, or are they interconnected? If they are interconnected, how are these connections addressed in your church's practice? For example, how are people suffering from illness or disability treated by your community?

3. How might Jesus' command to "cast out unclean spirits" be translated into practice in your church today? For example, consider the kinds of "demons" that might be said to "possess" people, such as homophobia, racism, or sexism; pursuit of material gain; violent nationalism; individualism; and so forth. What might it mean to "cast out" these spirits from people in your church or from the community as a whole?

4. How do outsiders come to know what your church believes and practices? Must they come "inside," or are there ways in which the life of the church goes "outside" in public witness? For example, is the church as a whole involved in community social or political issues, or are such things a matter of individual choice? Consider such collective stands taken by some church communities as:

- housing the homeless
- providing sanctuary for immigrants
- conducting public prayer services for an end to specific forms of violence or injustice
- engaging in a "sister parish" relationship with a church in an oppressed place
- contributing funds to support victims of natural disasters or political repression

How might your community respond to an invitation to these or other kinds of acts of collective witness?

6

The Early *Ekklēsia* Today

An Experimental Model for Discussion and Prayer

It is obvious that we cannot go back in time to recreate in our world the life of the first *ekklēsiai*. Similarly, we should not succumb to the temptation to romanticize the early discipleship communities, who, like their predecessors in Israel, often struggled and failed to remain faithful to God's ways amidst the pressures of empire. But I do believe that this exercise in recalling our origins as church can bear fruit for us. If nothing else, perhaps this reflection provides some response to the statements with which this book began about boring liturgy, authoritarian leadership, and so forth. The church was intended to be a social and economic space in which members' lives are intertwined both with each other and with the joyous gift of the Spirit's presence. It was to be a loving community in which differences among people that gave to some persons power over others were wiped out in the spirit of jubilee. It was to draw people into its orbit not with false promises or glitzy schemes but with the Good News of God's invitation to covenant life in the midst of a surrounding culture of death.

But I also believe that there is more to learn from our ancestors in faith than this. As we have seen, Acts, Revelation, and other texts portray the church as an integrated society struggling to live as free as possible from the controlling influence of empire. Not in the desert, but right in the middle of urban centers, were the churches to carve out their alternative way of life. I have no blue-prints for how this could be done today. But I have been inspired by numerous communities and projects around the nation in which I've seen a piece of this New Testament vision lived out. What follows in this chapter is offered as an imaginative synthesis of some of these experiments in church to generate your own ideas of how we might incarnate the *ekklēsia* in new and life-giving ways in our time and places.

One of the greatest obstacles in being church today in accordance with New Testament images and stories is that our lives are fragmented into largely unconnected social groups. This is no accidental development, of course, but the predictable result of an individualistic society grounded primarily in corporate and governmental institutional security structures. We have church friends, work colleagues, neighbors, school associates, and so forth. Along with this social fragmentation comes a temporal fragmentation. Our social architecture often requires us to work far from where we live and to shop and recreate far from either of those. Time spent simply getting from one piece of our lives to another necessitates breaking our days up into little chunks that leave little room either for spontaneity or deepening of relationships within any of our social circles. Flowing from these conditions is our utter inability to generate efficient and cooperative forms of economic interdependence. Living as we do, we must work longer hours to make enough money to produce absurdly duplicative resources, each household containing its own cooking, cleaning, and transportation devices and so forth. It seems virtually impossible from within this web to imagine living church truly as family members who share all things in common.

That is why the first step in reimagining church today in light of our foundational texts must be to present options for untangling ourselves from this web. The most obvious and yet perhaps most challenging means of taking this step is to provide a context in which all of the basic components of church life are found in one primary geographic and social location. Such a context would need to offer relative economic self-dependence so that members could work, live, worship and play in one place. The model that has lived within my own imagination for some time sees this being born at a rural school/farm/retreat center/worship space physically apart from but still related to a nearby urban center. Let's look at the pieces one at a time, understanding that they are necessarily components of an integrated whole.

A School for "Going Feral"

As noted earlier, most mainline Christians today do not come equipped with the basic skills of biblical and theological literacy. In the absence of intimate familiarity with the stories of scripture and subsequent Christian history, we are even more easily seduced into accepting imperial propaganda as a divinely inspired image of reality. We saw in chapter 2 how Bible study was meant to be an integral part of church life. Most programs offering Bible study in our society, though, suffer from one or more of the following limitations: (1) they focus on "personal spirituality" to the detriment of developing consciousness of the social, political, and economic contexts of the biblical texts; (2) they are offered as part of "professional ministry" training at universities and seminaries and thus are both very expensive and available only to an already highly educated few; (3) they take place within groups of randomly gathered individuals from local churches whose lives are not otherwise connected in ways that invite living out together what has been studied; or (4) they are available only in race- or class-specific contexts, denying the opportunity for cross-cultural and cross-class interpretation.

Biblical and theological literacy should be taught and practiced in a situation where students' lives, in all their diversity, intersect daily, not simply once a week a few times a year. It should also not be offered in isolation from other skills necessary to becoming church in old ways. For instance, most urban dwellers wouldn't begin to know how to find food apart from the grocery store, thus remaining utterly dependent on disintegrating aspects of urban geography. Similarly, most of us are totally dependent on "experts" for such basic skills as fixing our plumbing or electrical systems. The church should see as part of its mandate offering such skills that enable people to begin the process of "going feral," a term I first heard used by Ched Myers for reimagining ourselves as the "wild" creatures of our untamed Creator rather than as domesticated subjects of empire. Just as Latin American pedagogue Paolo Freire taught ordinary literacy to peasant farmers right in the midst of their daily work on the land, so could the church combine a program of biblical literacy with the tools for living which most of us don't have. In other words, hearing the biblical story with *new ears* calls for the practicing of God's ways with *new hands and feet*.

In this context, the process of text engagement itself would be transformed. For many people today, the biblical world can seem very distant and can therefore generate a powerful sense of alienation when first encountered. This can in turn lead to the dependence on "experts," whether clergy, professors, or other "certified" people. But as we've seen, the biblical stories were meant to empower ordinary folks, both rich and poor, to gain the vision and courage to be transformed by the Holy Spirit. Bible study and other forms of theological animation conducted *in the midst* of life rather than apart from life enable this kind of transformation to take place. People who are engaged in the struggle to live differently hear the biblical texts differently. Insights flow not out of academic expertise but from daily life experience.

In a world where priests or ministers provided such education, payment took the form of financial offerings to the church budget. Academic education is even more blatantly a commercial "product." In contrast, a "school for going feral" within the church would provide education for "residents" in exchange for contributed labor of one kind or another. Although we may lack food production and infrastructure repair ability, most of us come with something to offer that would be needed in the transformed church: accounting, cooking, teaching, physical labor, and so forth. In accordance with Pauline teachings, there would be no hierarchy among these various works. Each would contribute what they could to assure the abundant flow of what was needed for each and all.

The school would also provide a sort of mission work in offering weekend or weeklong immersion programs for urban dwellers not ready to join the *ekklēsia* full time but still interested in one or another of the educational programs. This could include offering skills to low-income persons or inner-city youth who are stuck in the cycle of poverty and violence endemic to much urban reality. In doing this, it would also carry out the traditional church function of offering "sanctuary" for those subject to imperial violence.

For the more wealthy, programs would be offered in exchange for payment of tuition which would pay for materials and tools that the *ekklēsia* could not fully produce on its own. As in the best forms of existing church stewardship, such payment would not simply buy an educational product; it would contribute to the welfare of the entire life of the church. In addition, this would furnish a link between the *ekklēsia* and the wider society, similar to the way the urban synagogue and the *ekklēsia* attracted "God-fearers" who were inspired by the life and work of the community but didn't feel called to join at that time. Thus, the school—in coordination with the other aspects described below—would begin a process of forging a chain of solidarity between rich and poor, members and nonmembers, urban and rural, through shared experiences and dialogue.

Beginning to Recover Food and Energy Self-sufficiency

There have been many efforts in recent decades to recover skills of organic gardening among urban dwellers. Pea patches and community-supported agriculture (CSA) have sprung up in many cities to reconnect people to the land and people from whom their food comes. These are not simply romantic, back-to-the-earth fantasies, but practical responses to the social and economic havoc wreaked by the current system of globalized food production and distribution. Growing consciousness of the downsides of this system—such as topsoil destruction, unanticipated ecological disruptions due to monoculture and genetic engineering, and the global spread of formerly local diseases—is even pushing some national governments to call for the relearning of local practices of sustainable agriculture

The *ekklēsia*, too, has much to learn from these movements. Organic, community-based agriculture may sound exotic to many, but it offers nothing more or less than the way most people have produced their food throughout history. Our captivity by propaganda is evident in our acceptance of globalized agriculture and its "conquest" of seasonal and geographic food diversity as "normal." The *ekklēsia* must return to its place at the forefront of building community literally from the ground up. As we have seen, the first thing the newly formed people of Israel did after escaping from Egypt was to establish a system of local food production. Their wilderness experience taught them to accept God's "daily bread" rather than to continue to rely on the imperial system of surplus left behind in Egypt. Similarly, Acts narrates the selling of private fields for the common good of the *ekklēsia*. Although Acts does not narrate the disciples engaged in farming, it seems reasonable to infer that the mention of fields in addition to houses (Acts 4:34) suggests that this must have been the case. Rome's economic power was built on its control of Egyptian and other grain production zones. For the *ekklēsia* to struggle toward freedom from imperial control, it must begin to teach people how to provide for our own food.

The agricultural aspect of the renewed *ekklēsia* would not be separate from the educational component discussed above. It is one thing for city people to grow a few rows of veggies in their yard and another to learn skills of production for a few hundred people. The explosion of interest in "sustainable agriculture" shows, however, that an ever-widening network of information, skills, and experience is available for those wanting to move the church in this direction. Increasing demand by ordinary people for healthy food free of genetic engineering and pesticides provides further impetus for incorporating this joyous function into the life of the *ekklēsia*. A CSA model is a simple and tested means with which to gain support for such a project by encouraging the participation of neighbors and others. In a CSA, people pay in advance for a share of the harvest. If there is a bumper crop, they share in the bounty. If there is a bad year, they share in the risk. The experience of CSAs to date has shown how remarkable relationships between producers and consumers can be formed which are impossible in the context of corporate food production. In my own region, the Tacoma Catholic Worker community has turned this into an art form in their Guadalupe Gardens. Not only do they produce large quantities of beautiful produce on otherwise abandoned inner-city lots; they bring in "subscribers" from other parts of town to meet the workers, who are often homeless people receiving a livable wage for their work. On a larger scale, such a farm could become the centerpiece of the life of the *ekklēsia*. Many of our urban poor, like their predecessors in the Greco-Roman cities, have been pushed by war or the global economy off their land. But before they were refugees or "undocumented" workers, they were farmers with the skills and experience of agricultural self-sufficiency. We of the U.S. middle class have much to learn in this regard from the poor. A school for going feral would provide the opportunity for this education to take place.

Many religious communities have learned how to support themselves in part by selling to the public the works of their hands and of the earth. Similarly, the *ekklēsia* would not only sell raw produce through a CSA; it could offer a line of "value added" products that extend the skills base of the community. Easy-to-produce items such as jam, salsa, cheese, and so forth would continue the process of developing a relatively self-sustaining economy, as generations of vowed Catholic religious communities have done. There is no reason why the *ekklēsia* could not become a source of a full line of organic foods and other earth-based products, created by workers living in community in a context of mutual learning and prayer.

A perhaps greater challenge in our time, but an equally necessary one, is developing some measure of energy independence. Perceived captivity to global, corporatized systems of fossil fuel production have led far too many Christians to remain silently powerless in the face of the environmental destruction and wars waged in defense of such systems. As with global food production, we are increasingly seeing revealed to us the ugly side-effects of this dependence. Specific abuses (oil spills, the Gulf War, manipulative rate setting) may be protested for a time, but little church-based organizing has been put into the deeper call to trust in the abundance of local energy provided by our God.

Economists such as Richard Douthwaite and Amory Lovins have applied hard-nosed thinking to the possibilities of traditional renewable energy sources such as wind, sun, and biomass being produced through local site "distributed utilities." Such renewable and inherently local systems can begin to restore control of energy resources to local communities as well as provide a more healthful environment for all creation. Lovins in particular has shown how an ordinary family home can, with existing technology, become a net energy producer rather than consumer. Impending breakthroughs in technologies such as hydrogen fuel cells and ultraefficient Stirling engines offer further hope for the capacity of local communities eventually to become free of the imperial power grid. There are numerous examples, rarely reported in mainstream media, of local communities seeking to develop such renewable systems. For example, Holden Village, a Christian renewal center in Washington state's Cascade Mountains, supplies energy for over five hundred summer staff and guests from a small hydroelectric plant on a local creek. A community in Brazil has shown enormous creativity in collecting the energy of children on teeter-totters into water-driven turbines!

Again, our sisters and brothers whose first home was in Latin American, Asian, or African villages "off the grid" have the basic energy-generating skills many of us First World–born folks do not. Of course, this also means learning to live more simply with regard to energy and other patterns of consumption. Living, working, worshiping, and playing in one place can generate enormous energy efficiencies, including greatly reduced travel-fuel needs, use of common space, and so forth. Good earth stewardship as well as the call to "come out of empire" push the *ekklēsia* to be at the forefront of this movement. While there are many denominational and ecumenical organizations working for sustainable energy development, there have been few local churches who see this as part of their mission *right where they live*. There is no reason why the *ekklēsia* cannot become a model both for sensible conservation of limited earth resources and for developing the skills of local energy production.

A Place for Sabbath and Refreshment

Conventional churches today already know how great is the need among stressed city people for times of retreat and renewal. Centers such as Holden Village in the Cascade Mountains of Washington state or the Center for Action and Contemplation in the New Mexico desert have long offered such gifts in wilderness settings of natural beauty and simplicity. Church newspapers and magazines are filled with advertisements for retreat centers with excellent programs. However, most of these places are still largely dependent on the dominant culture's systems of resource and wealth production. In other words, people come for a moment of refreshment only to feed their renewed energy back into "the matrix." Similarly, without empire's wealth—whether in the form of individual fees, foundation grants, or donations—many of these places would quickly go out of business.

Being faithful to our founding vision calls for us to integrate such experiences of renewal into the lives and structures of local *ekklēsiai.* This means, in coordination with the food and energy ministries discussed above, rethinking where discipleship communities find their primary location. The dichotomy between urban and rural, between temple and wilderness, must be broken down in favor of more hybrid spaces that offer both access and refreshment. This is certainly at the heart of Revelation's vision of New Jerusalem, in which the Holy City is imbued with both refreshing river and abundant, fruit-bearing trees. Our call is to relearn the weaving together of human and natural spaces so that sabbath-taking, like food growing and production, can take place amidst, rather than apart from, church life.

In addition to offering retreats, workshops, and other more familiar renewal ministries, the *ekklēsia* could also become a place of sabbatical for those in transition of one kind or another. At one end of the spectrum of need are people who have lost jobs, been victims of domestic or family violence, or otherwise are in situations in life where conventional society offers little support. The institutionalization of government-sponsored social services such as homeless shelters, detox facilities, and so forth removes treatment from the life of a supportive community of prayer which seeks, in accordance with the gospel, to provide healing for the whole person. The dehumanizing experience of having to apply to a bureaucracy to obtain the most basic life resources is one the *ekklēsia* should find intolerable. Denominational charity agencies such as Lutheran or Catholic Relief Services have done excellent work in bringing the commitment of church people to bear on these pressing needs. But they largely remain apart from the daily life of the church members who sponsor them, having become institutional bureaucracies of their own. More local, church-based programs such as domestic violence shelters are often staffed by deeply compassionate and committed persons who accept low pay for important work, and then are left to figure out how to avoid homelessness themselves in the face of the limited supply of affordable housing in many cities today.

The kind of *ekklēsia* I am describing ought to be a place where such people in need and those with skills to serve them can come together in a natural embrace. Rather than isolating people who are in pain, the *ekklēsia,* in the spirit of Jesus, would offer a healing presence that would help people experience God's love rather than an institutional mat or handout. Further, the integration of people in need within the faith community would incarnate the true meaning of Jesus' often misunderstood words, "the poor you have with you always." Jesus was not expressing a cynical acceptance of the unending fact of poverty, but rather the *ekklēsia*'s call to include the poor *as part of the community*.

This was a principle well understood by people such as Dorothy Day, the founder of the Catholic Worker movement. Many Worker communities have struggled with this challenge, because the abuse of the poor has often meant that they lack the social skills important to the healthy functioning of a community. For example, group process tools such as effective listening, constructive uses of power and leadership, and conflict resolution procedures are vital to the life of any intimate group. However, the struggle simply to survive in a hostile and violent world has left most of the poor without any access to such tools. Thus, in the context of a tiny community such as a Catholic Worker house, it can seem an impossible burden on the poor to include them in the decision-making process of the community. In a larger *ekklēsia*, however, those in need of healing could come simply to be healed and to do the work they *can* do, rather than be pressured to do what they cannot do. This mode has worked well in models such as Jean Vanier's L'Arche communities, where people with developmental disabilities live in prayerful, celebratory communities along with differently abled folk. There ought be no limit on this kind of imaginative partnering within the *ekklēsia* without expecting people to be other than what they are or can be, while at the same time expanding our sense of the giftedness of each person.

In addition to providing a safe and nurturing sanctuary for those at the oppressed margins of the dominant society, the *ekklēsia* could serve as a sabbatical place for artists, musicians, scholars, and other creative persons, as it once did in monasteries. In our world, artists so often find themselves caught choosing between maintaining creative integrity and making a living. Whether through the inducements of corporate-generated mass culture or the competition for foundation grants, the divinely inspired gifts given to creative people of faith are often reduced to what sells or is acceptable to cultural arbiters. Instead of remaining stuck in this system, artists and scholars could again become an integral part of the life of the *ekklēsia* as they listen and respond to God's call to them to give imaginative expression to life. The fruits of their labors would enrich the *ekklēsia* and its visitors just as importantly as the fruits of the earthly harvest. As Israel understood the tribe of Levi to be denied its own allotment of land in exchange for their priestly service, so the *ekklēsia* could support people whose vocation may be to other forms of productivity. For, of course, Jesus recognized that people do not live on bread alone, but on the mixture of both physical and spiritual food.

"Holy, Holy, Holy": The Heart of the Ekklēsia's *Life*

In presenting this thought experiment in a re-formed *ekklēsia*, I have reversed the usual order of assumptions about the Christian communal life. This book started with the recognition that for most people, the *only* aspect of church life they experience is Sunday worship. The challenge has been to show how the first *ekklēsia* was a holistic enterprise, incorporating all the tasks and functions important to a healthy community of God's people. Now we conclude where we started: with a renewed sense of the role of the church's worship.

Liturgy, in the words of Jack Morris, S.J., is "a holy waste of time." It is not "productive" in the way that a farm or even an artist is. There is no "thing" left at the completion of worship. Yet, to its credit, the church has long known that this "waste of time" is the center point for a life rooted in God's abundant love. I have often heard people complain about worship services that lasted longer than the expected hour: "there is work to do, we can't just sit around here all day and pray!" But in the *ekklēsia* as intended by Jesus, the sabbath day would again be honored and enjoyed as a full, weekly cycle of rest, prayer, re-creation, and celebration. Far from the "Sunday obligation" which brings some dutifully to church, true worship would draw people like bees to a flowery meadow. There ought be no more joyous occasion than the people of God gathered in praise and petition. As we saw in chapter 2, Revelation shows us prayer and worship "on the other side of the veil" consisting of a tremendous outpouring of incense, song, and cheering for God's ongoing victory over empire and provision of all good things. It is easy for me to envision Sunday worship in the *ekklēsia* celebrated in the context of an ongoing banquet from morning until night in which people could come and go as the Spirit moved them. A blend of the formal and the spontaneous, the traditional with the freshly creative, would offer rich fare for hungry pilgrims on the Way.

In addition, throughout the week, worship would frame the life of the *ekklēsia*. Morning matins and evening vespers would encircle each day's labors with praise and thanksgiving for the gifts received and shared. Some might feel called to leadership in this aspect of the church's life and be commissioned as such by the whole congregation. Others might express their gifts from time to time without feeling a call to a lifetime vocation in liturgical service. A deep listening to the Spirit would help the *ekklēsia* to make these kinds of decisions, not a rigid adherence to historical forms. Just as Jesus saw his ministry to fulfill, not to abolish, the Torah, the renewed *ekklēsia* would not abandon centuries of tradition but would allow it to be freshly invigorated by God's own Spirit. The Catholic renewal process of Vatican II is a recent and well-known example of how the old and new can work together in harmony. Numerous powerful, yet lesser known movements throughout church history have also attempted such old-new syntheses, such as the twelfth-century Franciscans or the thirteenth-century women's community the Beguines.

What is true about the church's prayer and worship is thus true about the larger life of the church as well. We thrive best when learning from the experience of our ancestors in faith while at the same time remaining open to the workings of the Spirit. It is perhaps ironic that the most radical thing the church today could do is also deeply conservative: to recover the most ancient teachings and practices of the first discipleship communities. Numerous Protestant denominations have been spawned over the centuries in an effort to do this. Yet I believe that the challenge today is not for a new "Reformation" but for a revitalization of existing Christian traditions, both Catholic and Protestant, by the recovery of our founding stories and the adventures in discipleship that they reflect and advocate. Catholics branded by some as "reactionaries" because they yearn for the "old" church prior to Vatican II may find themselves even more challenged by the truly "old" church than by the one experienced simply in previous decades. Those Catholics seen as "liberals" may themselves be disturbed by the kind of deep and uncompromising commitment that worship of "YHWH alone" can mean in a pluralistic society. Protestants languishing in declining mainline congregations may equally find the recovery of ancient tradition deeply threatening to familiar but often uninspiring church practice. From wherever one stands on the spectrum of tradition and change, it can be a bracing experience to consider the true vocation of the *ekklēsia*. But if we are truly seeking to live as God's people, as people trusting in the Good News of Jesus and in the presence of the Holy Spirit, we might do well to do our own imagining of how the faith lived by our ancestors can continue to guide us today. Perhaps through our reflection, study, prayer, and conversation, we can together as church hear once again the Spirit which "over the bent World broods with warm breast & with ah! bright wings."*

---

*Gerard Manley Hopkins, S.J., "God's Grandeur."

Reflection Questions

1. Imagine what you would consider to be the "perfect" church. How would it be similar to or different from the kind of church you now experience? How would it compare to the models of *ekklēsia* examined in this book?

2. What are the tasks for which you rely on "experts" to get the job done? Consider one such expertise that you might develop for yourself. What would be different if you and/or your church thought of these activities as "ministry"?

3. Consider the sources of the food you eat and the energy you consume. What value system(s) underlie their production and distribution? What would change if you imagined those functions to be "sacred" acts?

4. What do you do and where do you go to find spiritual refreshment? Is it apart from or integrated into the rest of your life? How might you imagine a church community incorporating *play* into its life?

Selected Bibliography

Albertz, Rainer. *A History of Israelite Religion in the Old Testament Period*. 2 volumes. Louisville: Westminster/John Knox Press, 1994.

Alternative Farming Systems Information Center and the Sustainable Agriculture Network. *Database of Community Supported Agriculture in the United States* (http://www.nal.usda.gov/afsic/csa/csastate.htm).

Banks, Robert. *Paul's Idea of Community*. Revised edition. Peabody, Mass.: Hendrickson, 1994.

Brown, Raymond E. *The Churches the Apostles Left Behind*. New York: Paulist, 1984.

Collins, John J. *Between Athens and Jerusalem: Jewish Identity in the Hellenistic Diaspora*. Grand Rapids: Eerdmans, 1999.

Crosby, Michael. *House of Disciples: Church, Economics, and Justice in Matthew*. Maryknoll, N.Y.: Orbis, 1988.

Cross, Frank Moore. *From Epic to Canon: History and Literature in Ancient Israel*. Baltimore and London: Johns Hopkins University Press, 1998.

Cwiekowski, Frederick J. *The Beginnings of the Church*. New York: Paulist, 1988.

Douthwaite, Richard. *Short Circuit: Strengthening Local Economics for Security in an Unstable World*. White River Junction, Vt.: Chelsea Green Publishing, 1998.

Eisenberg, Evan. *The Ecology of Eden*. New York: Vintage, 1999.

Elliott, Neil. *Liberating Paul: The Justice of God and the Politics of the Apostle*. Maryknoll, N.Y.: Orbis, 1995).

Ferguson, John. *The Religions of the Roman Empire*. Ithaca, N.Y.: Cornell University Press, 1970.

Freire, Pablo. *Pedagogy of the Oppressed.* 30th anniversary edition. New York: Continuum, 2000.

Goodman, Martin. *Mission and Conversion: Proselytizing in the Religious History of the Roman Empire.* Oxford: Clarendon, 1994.

Gottwald, Norman. *The Politics of Ancient Israel.* Louisville: Westminster/John Knox Press, 2001.

———. *The Tribes of Yahweh.* Maryknoll, N.Y.: Orbis, 1979.

Hawken, Paul, Amory Lovins, and L. Hunter Lovins. *Natural Capitalism: Creating the Next Industrial Revolution.* Boston: Back Bay Books, 2000.

Horsley, Richard A., ed. *Paul and Empire: Religion and Power in Roman Imperial Society.* Harrisburg, Pa.: Trinity Press International, 1997.

Horsley, Richard A., and John S. Hanson. *Bandits, Prophets and Messiahs: Popular Movements at the Time of Jesus.* Harrisburg, Pa.: Trinity Press International, 1999.

Howard-Brook, Wes. *John's Gospel and the Renewal of the Church.* Maryknoll, N.Y.: Orbis, 1997.

———, and Anthony Gwyther. *Unveiling Empire: Reading Revelation Then and Now.* Maryknoll, N.Y.: Orbis, 1999.

Lovins, Amory, and Chris Lotspeich. "Energy Surprises for the 21st Century." *Journal of International Affairs* (fall 1999): 53. Also available at http://www.rmi.org/images/other/E-EnergySurprises.pdf.

MacMullen, Ramsey. *Roman Social Relations, 50 BC to AD 284.* New Haven and London: Yale University Press, 1974.

Malherbe, Abraham J. *Social Aspects of Early Christianity.* 2nd edition. Philadelphia: Fortress, 1983.

Malina, Bruce J. *The New Testament World: Insights from Cultural Anthropology.* Atlanta: John Knox, 1981.

Meeks, Wayne A. *The First Urban Christians: The Social World of the Apostle Paul.* New Haven and London: Yale University Press, 1983.

Meyers, Carol. *Discovering Eve: Ancient Israelite Women in Context.* New York: Oxford University Press, 1988.

Miller, Patrick D. *The Religion of Ancient Israel.* Louisville: Westminster/John Knox, 2000.

Myers, Ched. *Binding the Strong Man: A Political Reading of Mark's Story of Jesus.* Maryknoll, N.Y.: Orbis, 1988.

———. *"Say To This Mountain."* Maryknoll, N.Y.: Orbis, 1994.

Perdue, Leo, Joseph Blenkinsopp, John J. Collins, and Carol L. Meyers.

Families in Ancient Israel. Louisville: Westminster/John Knox Press, 1997.

Sternberg, Meir. *The Poetics of Biblical Narrative: Ideological Literature and the Drama of Reading.* Indianapolis: Indiana University Press, 1984.

Vanier, Jean. *Community and Growth.* Revised edition. New York: Paulist, 1999.

Wink, Walter. *Engaging the Powers: Discernment and Resistance in a World of Domination.* Philadelphia: Fortress, 1992.

Scripture Index

New Testament